selected prayers

ADAPTED AND THEMED FOR PUBLIC WORSHIP

selected prayers
ADAPTED AND THEMED FOR
PUBLIC WORSHIP

nick FAWCETT

kevin
mayhew

First published in 2003 by

KEVIN MAYHEW LTD
Buxhall, Stowmarket, Suffolk, IP14 3BW
E-mail: info@kevinmayhewltd.com

KINGSGATE PUBLISHING INC
1000 Pannell Street, Suite G, Columbia, MO 65201
E-mail: sales@kingsgatepublishing.com

9 8 7 6 5 4 3 2 1 0

ISBN 1 84417 070 5
Catalogue No 1500586

Cover design by Angela Selfe
Typesetting by Louise Selfe
Printed in Great Britain

Contents

Foreword

During my early years in the pastoral ministry, I followed the time-honoured tradition among nonconformists of long and wide-ranging extemporary prayers. There is nothing wrong with extemporary prayer, of course – on the contrary, it can have an immediacy that written prayers sometimes lack – but the issue of length, together with the array of issues covered, can be a problem. On occasions, listening to a particularly loquacious offering, I have felt myself starting to nod off, or else wondering just who or what else there could be left to pray for! Anxious to avoid such pitfalls when leading prayer, I increasingly found myself drawn to focusing simply (and hopefully succinctly) on specific issues relating to daily life and faith, typically putting together two or three prayers on a related theme. Sometimes I would write these myself; at other times I would make use of already published material. The trouble with the latter approach – apart from the very real problem of finding prayers that came across as natural – was that I often entered the pulpit weighed down by a collection of prayer books, having chosen one prayer from each. Switching smoothly from one book to another was not always easy, and a bookmark slipping out from between the pages could spell disaster. What I really needed (but never found) was a single-volume collection drawing together from their various sources all the prayers that had proven or might prove useful.

Such a consideration lies behind this book. Having recently compiled a collection of short prayers for public worship, it occurred to me that a similar compilation of slightly longer prayers from the many books I have written (such as *No Ordinary Man 1* and *2*, *The Unfolding Story*, *Daily Prayer*, and a range of Bible study booklets) might prove useful. A number of these prayers were originally linked to service orders, quiet days or particular studies, often to be found in appendices at the back of the book in question. Others were designed initially for personal devotion or small-group use rather than for public worship. I have brought these various strands together here, adapting and revising the prayers as necessary and arranging them for ease of use into themed sections covering key seasons of the Christian year and various aspects of Christian discipleship. I hope that this selection might prove useful in helping to integrate prayer with the reading and exposition of Scripture and with other aspects of public worship. If it succeeds in doing so, then the time involved in collating it will have been well spent.

NICK FAWCETT

———— Adversity, faith in ————

see also Discipleship, journey of; Faithfulness of God; Hope and despair

1

Gracious God,
  you came to our world through Jesus Christ,
  and, despite everything that conspires against you,
  your love continues to shine through him.
You conquered the forces of evil,
  you overcame the sting of death,
  and you brought joy out of sorrow,
  hope out of despair.
Teach us, whatever we may face,
  to hold on to that truth,
  confident that you will always lead us out of darkness
  into your marvellous light.
Hold on to us when life is hard,
  and assure us that you are present even in the bleakest moments,
  able to use every moment of each day
  in ways beyond our imagining.
Amen.

2

Living God,
  there are times when we find it hard to make sense of life
  and when your purpose is difficult to fathom.
We are puzzled by our experiences,
  confused by so much that seems to contradict your will
  and deny your love,
  and we wonder why you seem so distant,
  so unconcerned about our needs.
Yet experience has taught us
  that you are often at work in ways we do not recognise,
  responding to our cry and guiding our steps,
  even though we have no inkling of it at the time.
You have been with us in the darkest moments,
  holding on to us even when we do not see your hand.
May that truth inspire us whenever life proves testing in the future,
  so that, however far away you may seem,
  we will know that you are near,
  and stride out in that confidence,
  through Jesus Christ our Lord.
Amen.

3
Loving God,
  we don't like failing at something.
It hurts our pride,
  destroys our confidence
  and undermines our self-esteem.
Far better, we tell ourselves, to cut our losses,
  admit defeat,
  and focus on the things we know we can do well.
Yet you have shown so often through your people
  that success is not always won easily;
  that there are times when we must work for it despite setbacks,
  persevering come what may.
Teach us, then, never to lose heart,
  but to take the leap of faith in times of adversity,
  confident that ultimately the victory will be yours
  through Christ our Saviour.
Amen.

4
Living God,
  we like to think that we are the world's survivors,
  able to meet whatever life may throw at us and emerge unscathed,
  but, in our hearts of hearts,
  we know that we are as vulnerable as the next person,
  our composure and confidence hanging on a thread
  that can be broken at any time.
A crisis,
  difficulty,
  disappointment
  or personal tragedy,
  and the whole edifice we have so carefully constructed
  can come tumbling down around our ears.
Most of the time we succeed in shutting out such thoughts,
  finding them too uncomfortable to contemplate,
  but sometimes they force their way into our consciousness,
  and we can escape them no longer.
Save us from running away in a vain attempt to deny the truth;
  from taking a road that leads only to uncertainty mounting
  and fear gaining an ever-firmer hold.
Teach us instead to share our burdens and anxieties with you,
  and so to find strength,
  peace,
  hope
  and courage,

even when the storm rages about us,
   secure in the knowledge of your eternal love
   made known through Jesus Christ our Lord.
Amen.

5
Lord,
   it's easy to follow you when life is going well;
   much harder when we come up against problems.
Forgive us for the weakness of our faith,
   for being fair-weather disciples,
   swift to turn back when the going gets rough.
Help us to recognise that there are times when we must face challenges
   and overcome apparently insurmountable obstacles,
   and teach us that you are as much with us in those times as at any other.
Give us courage to walk wherever you lead,
   confident that you will never forsake us.
Amen.

6
Lord,
   it's hard to keep striving sometimes when all our efforts meet with failure;
   hard to keep praying when all our prayers seem to be unanswered;
   hard to keep believing when so much in life seems to undermine our faith.
Yet it is at such times as those that we need to hold firmly to you,
   discovering the strength that you alone can give
   and trusting in your sovereign purpose.
Teach us to persevere
   even when the odds seem hopelessly stacked against us,
   confident that your will shall finally prevail
   despite everything that conspires against it.
Help us to know that though we may be tempted to give up on you,
   you will never give up on us!
Amen.

7
Sovereign God,
   it is easy to trust you when life is good,
   but when circumstances change, then faith is suddenly put to the test.
When one problem,
   one anxiety,
   one sorrow follows another,
   we feel overwhelmed,
   swimming against a current that sweeps us deeper and deeper into difficulty.

Teach us that however fierce the storm,
    it can never finally swamp us,
    for you will be there to rescue us in our time of need.
Teach us to hold firmly to you
    knowing that you will keep hold of us
    until the storm is past and calm returns.
In Jesus' name we pray.
Amen.

8

Gracious God,
    when life is testing and your purpose is hard to fathom,
    help us to remember that you are able to see us through.
When we feel overwhelmed by the challenge before us,
    yet see nowhere and no one to turn to,
    remind us to reach out to you,
    knowing that whenever we need you,
    you will be there.
Teach us that, with you, no situation is beyond hope,
    and that no darkness can ever fully extinguish the light,
    and in that confidence may we walk each day in faith,
    to the glory of your name.
Amen.

Call of God

see also Guidance; Prayer

9

Gracious God,
    we thank you that you have spoken throughout history,
    calling people to your service.
We thank you for those who have had the courage to respond,
    even when that call has involved unpopularity,
    ridicule and persecution.
We thank you that these were ordinary everyday people,
    just like us:
    hesitant,
    fearful,
    uncertain of their ability to do what you asked of them,
    yet receiving the strength they needed when they needed it.
Still today you call your people to challenging areas of service –
    to jobs they would rather not do,
    issues they would rather not face
    and messages they would rather not deliver.
Yet, once again, you promise that you will give each one of your people
    the resources they need to meet the task.
Give us, then, courage to hear your voice
    and to respond to your call,
    through Jesus Christ our Lord.
Amen.

10

Living God,
    we praise you that you have called us to faith in Christ,
    to fellowship in your Church,
    to Christian discipleship.
We praise you that you keep on calling us
    to new avenues of service,
    new ways of serving you,
    new ways of working towards your kingdom.
Forgive us that we are sometimes slow or unwilling to respond:
    we do not always understand what you are asking of us,
    we resist when your call is too demanding,
    we run from that which we would rather not do.
Thank you that though we ignore or disobey your call,
    still you seek us out,
    gently and lovingly leading us back to your way

and entrusting to us,
despite our faithlessness,
the message of the gospel.
Thank you for being a God full of mercy:
slow to anger,
abounding in steadfast love,
your nature always to forgive –
a God who is always ready to give a second chance,
repeatedly showing your patience,
demonstrating your awesome grace time and time again.
Help us to hear your voice clearly,
to accept your will humbly
and to respond to it gladly.
We ask it in the name of Christ.
Amen.

11
Lord,
you do not call us all to positions of eye-catching responsibility,
but we each have a part to play in your service nonetheless.
Whatever our gifts,
we have a contribution to make
that you can use in fulfilling something of your eternal purpose.
Teach us, then, to listen for your voice,
and, when you call,
to respond gladly,
offering whatever you ask whenever you need it,
to the glory of your name.
Amen.

12
Sovereign God,
you spoke and the universe was created:
the heavens and the earth,
the night and day,
the sea and dry land –
life in all its bewildering variety and beauty.
You spoke again,
and your people heard your voice –
Abraham, Isaac and Jacob,
Moses, Joshua, Elijah,
kings, priests, judges, prophets –
an ever-growing succession of those who listened to your word
and responded to your call.
You spoke in Christ,
your call coming once more –

to shepherds and magi,
tax-collectors and sinners,
rich and poor,
men and women –
your word bringing light and hope,
joy and life.
You speak still –
to us,
to all –
offering your mercy, wholeness and renewal,
but calling also to loving service and bold witness.
Help us, like those before us, to respond in faith,
ready to follow where you may lead,
working for the growth of your kingdom
and the glory of your name.
In the name of Christ we pray.
Amen.

13

Loving God,
we thank you for your call:
to discipleship, fellowship and service;
to sharing as your people in the work of your kingdom.
We thank you that you call us as we are,
with all our faults, weaknesses and doubts,
accepting us not through our own deserving,
but through your grace,
your love,
and your mercy.
Above all, we thank you for the inner presence of your Holy Spirit,
through which Christ is constantly at work within us,
moving deep within to change our lives
and to draw us ever closer to you.
Loving God,
receive our praise in his name.
Amen.

14

Lord Jesus Christ,
you speak your word to us
as you spoke it to the Apostles long ago:
'Come, follow me.'
You call us, as you have called so many over the years:
'Come to me,
all who are weary of carrying heavy burdens,
and I will give you rest.'

You offer us,
   as you offer all your people,
   refreshment for our souls,
   promising that anyone who is thirsty can come to you and drink.
Lord,
   we thank you for that invitation,
   and gladly we respond.
But, more than that, we thank you that before anyone comes to you,
   you come first to them.
You came to Peter, James and John by the lakeside;
   to the hungry, the sick and the outcasts in the streets of Galilee;
   to Mary Magdalene weeping in the garden;
   to two weary disciples walking the Emmaus Road;
   to the Apostles trembling behind locked doors;
   to Saul breathing murder on the road to Damascus;
   and so to countless others since.
Always it is you who makes the first approach,
   calling your people to faith,
   and still you come through your Spirit to meet with us.
Open our eyes to your presence
   and lead us forward in your service until that day when,
   with all your people,
   we enter your kingdom and meet you face to face.
In your name we ask it.
Amen.

15

Gracious God,
   you act in ways we do not expect,
   you speak in ways we do not always understand,
   you come at times and in places we least imagine,
   and all too easily we fail to recognise your presence amongst us.
Teach us to be awake to your prompting,
   however unlikely it may seem,
   and to respond whenever you call
   even though we have no idea where it might lead.
Equip us to walk in faith,
   through Jesus Christ our Lord.
Amen.

Voice of God

16

Loving God,
    forgive us for refusing sometimes to listen to your voice.
Deep down in our hearts of hearts we know you are speaking to us,
    but we would rather not hear.
When your message is too demanding,
    when you ask of us what we would rather not face,
    when your words make us feel uncomfortable,
    striking too near the mark,
    we stubbornly resist,
    closing our ears and pushing you away.
Yet however hard we may try,
    we will never finally silence your voice –
    not until we have listened and responded.
Help us, then, to hear what you would say to us,
    and act upon it.
Amen.

17

Loving God,
    there are times when,
    no matter how we call,
    you seem silent,
    when we cannot hear your voice
    no matter how we listen for it.
Grant us courage in those moments
    to ask if we have closed our hearts and minds
    to what you would say,
    but help us also to understand that there are times
    when you expect us to get on with the business of discipleship
    without you directing our every step.
Help us to see that your silence need not be a sign of our faithlessness
    or of your displeasure,
    but might rather point to your love,
    offering us the opportunity to grow towards Christian maturity.
Help us, then, to remember all those times you have spoken unmistakably,
    to us
    and to others,
    and let those moments sustain and direct us
    until your word comes again,
    in the name of Christ.
Amen.

Christian seasons

First Sunday of Advent

18

Lord Jesus Christ,
    we remember today that though your people longed for your coming,
    many were not prepared to welcome you,
    failing to recognise you when you came.
Forgive us that we are equally closed sometimes
    to your coming into our lives,
    forcing you into a mould we have made for you,
    presuming your thoughts and your ways are the same as ours.
Forgive us that our expectations are small and limited,
    shaped by looking at life from a human rather than eternal perspective.
Forgive us,
    and help us to be prepared.
Teach us to examine ourselves –
    our words and deeds,
    thoughts and attitudes –
    and so to live each day open to what you would do in us and through us,
    to the glory of your name.
Amen.

19

Lord Jesus Christ,
    we have come to worship you in this glad season of Advent,
    a season of expectation,
    of celebration,
    and, above all, of preparation.
We come now, because we want to be ready –
    ready to give thanks for your coming,
    to recognise the ways you come to us now,
    and to welcome you when you come again.
Open our hearts as we worship you,
    so that all we share may give us a deeper understanding of this season
    and a fuller experience of your love.
In his name we ask it.
Amen.

20

Lord Jesus Christ,
    as you came once, so you shall come again
    to establish your kingdom
    and to fulfil the purpose of the One who sent you.

Help us to learn from your first coming
   and to remember that,
   despite the long years of expectation
   and the desire of so many to see you,
   few found room for you when you finally came.
Save us, then, from complacency,
   and teach us to live each day to your glory,
   happy at each moment to stand in your presence
   and ready to welcome you on the day of your return.
In your name we pray.
Amen.

Second Sunday of Advent

21

Gracious God,
   your word was active from the beginning
   and shall continue until the end of time.
It brought life itself into existence,
   and controls the destiny of everything you have created.
What you have decreed shall be,
   for no word of yours returns to you empty.
Help us, then, to listen to what you would say to us
   both today and throughout this season of Advent.
Open our ears, our hearts and our minds,
   so that we may hear your voice and respond in joyful service,
   through Jesus Christ our Lord.
Amen.

22

Living God,
   you spoke,
   and the world was brought into being –
   the heavens and the earth,
   the sea and dry land,
   night and day,
   life in all its variety and abundance.
You spoke again in the book of the Law,
   the poetry of the psalms,
   the wisdom of the teacher,
   the chronicling of history
   and the message of the prophets,
   revealing your will,
   proclaiming your purpose.
You spoke through Jesus Christ, the Word made flesh,
   through those who witnessed to his life and ministry,

and through those who across the years have shared
  in the building of his Church.
You have spoken throughout history:
  through preaching and teaching,
  through study and quiet devotion,
  through prayer and fellowship,
  through the wonder of this world;
  and still you speak today,
  your word ever old but always new,
  able to redeem,
  renew and restore.
Speak to us now,
  we pray.
Help us to use this season of Advent
  to listen more carefully to your voice,
  and so to walk with you more closely,
  this and every day,
  through Jesus Christ our Lord.
Amen.

23
Loving God,
  we praise you that the light which dawned
  in the life of Zechariah and Elizabeth,
  that transformed the future for Mary and Joseph,
  and that lit up the sky on the night of the Saviour's birth,
  continues to shine today.
We thank you for the new beginning you have brought in our lives,
  and the light that continues to guide us.
Teach us to walk in that light day by day,
  and so may each moment be a new dawn,
  a new beginning,
  rich in promise and filled by your love,
  through Jesus Christ our Lord.
Amen.

24
Loving God,
  from earliest times you have been at work in our world,
  striving to fulfil your purposes,
  preparing the way for the coming of your kingdom.
We praise you for the witness of the prophets
  foretelling the coming of the Messiah.
We praise you for the ministry of John the Baptist,
  a voice in the wilderness calling people to repentance,
  making ready the way of the Lord.

We praise you for those who made the gospel known to us,
    giving us the opportunity to respond.
Help us now truly to prepare for Christmas,
    not simply outwardly but inwardly,
    so that we may joyfully celebrate the birth of Christ
    and receive him into our lives.
In his name we ask it.
Amen.

25
Lord Jesus Christ,
    you call us to test ourselves and to ensure that we are still in the faith.
Help us to take that challenge seriously,
    for we so easily imagine all is well when in fact much is wrong.
We talk of listening to your voice,
    but hear what we want to hear.
We speak of seeking your will,
    yet we prefer our way,
    expecting you to conform to our expectations.
Draw close to us and fill us with your Spirit,
    so that our faith may be as real and as fresh today
    as the moment we first believed.
Prepare us for your coming again,
    so that we may be ready to receive you
    and found faithful in your service,
    to the glory of your name.
Amen.

Third Sunday of Advent

26
Lord Jesus Christ,
    we thank you for all those who prepared the way for your coming,
    whether long ago in Bethlehem
    or in countless hearts since that day.
We think especially of John the Baptist,
    remembering his courage to speak the truth no matter what the cost,
    his readiness to point away from himself and towards your light,
    his willingness to live in such a way
    that everything he did testified to the truth of his message
    in a manner that words alone could never do.
Help us to prepare your way in turn,
    witnessing to your renewing power
    and demonstrating your compassion,
    so that the hearts of many may be made ready to receive you
    and to respond to your grace.

In your name we ask it.
Amen.

27

Gracious God,
   we come to reflect again on your age-old promises,
   on your sovereign purpose,
   on your constant working within human history.
We remember that you brought this world into being,
   that you guided your people across the centuries,
   despite repeated rebellion and disobedience,
   and that, through your great love,
   you took on human flesh,
   coming to our world through Jesus Christ.
We rejoice in all he showed of you
   through his birth in Bethlehem,
   through his life and ministry,
   through his death and resurrection,
   and we celebrate his living presence with us now through his Spirit.
Open our hearts to everything you would say to us through this day,
   so that we may understand your love more completely
   and serve you more faithfully,
   through Jesus Christ our Lord.
Amen.

28

Lord Jesus Christ,
   we remember today the ministry of John the Baptist:
   his readiness to spend himself in service,
   to proclaim the good news of your kingdom,
   to point away from himself
   and to seek your glory rather than his own.
Forgive us that we find it so hard to follow his example,
   preferring instead the way of self-service,
   of putting our own interests before those of others.
Help us to recognise that it is in giving that we receive,
   and so may we commit our lives to you
   and bring glory to your name.
Amen.

29

Sovereign God
   we thank you for all who have borne witness to your coming in Christ,
   all who have shared their faith

so that others might come to know him
and experience his love for themselves.
We thank you for those from whom we first heard the gospel,
and all who have nurtured and encouraged us in discipleship.
Help us now to play our part in that continuing ministry,
sharing what Christ means to those around us,
and making known the way he has worked in our lives.
Send us out in his name,
to his glory.
Amen.

30
Loving God,
we celebrate today the fulfilment of your word across the years.
You promised Abraham that through his offspring
all the earth would be blessed –
and it was.
You promised through your prophets that the Messiah would come –
and he came.
You promised Mary that she would give birth to a son –
and she did.
You promised the disciples that death would not be the end –
and it wasn't.
You promised your followers that they would receive the Holy Spirit –
and it happened.
Teach us, then, to trust you for the present and the future,
knowing that you are always faithful,
and that you will accomplish whatever you have pledged to do.
Teach us to be faithful to you in all our dealings,
just as you are invariably faithful to us.
In Christ's name we ask it.
Amen.

31
Lord Jesus Christ,
you promise that when two or three are gathered in your name,
you will be there among them.
Help us to trust in that promise –
to know you are here
and to meet with you now through the inner presence of your Holy Spirit.
Open our eyes to your presence,
speak again your word of life,
and help us to listen,
to believe
and to respond,
to the glory of your name.
Amen.

Fourth Sunday of Advent

32

Lord Jesus Christ,
  we know and love the message of Christmas so well,
  perhaps too well –
  for we have heard and celebrated it so many times
  and can imagine we have understood all it has to say to us.
Save us from that danger,
  and help us to reflect on what your coming means
  for us,
  for others,
  for all;
  for yesterday,
  today
  and tomorrow.
Speak to us now,
  through readings,
  through music,
  through prayer,
  through your Spirit at work within us.
Speak through all we shall share together,
  nurturing our faith,
  strengthening our commitment
  and expanding our love for you and for all.
In your name we ask it.
Amen.

33

Almighty God,
  you are greater than our minds can fathom,
  higher than our highest thoughts,
  sovereign over all,
  worthy of praise and honour.
Forgive us that we sometimes lose
  our sense of awe and wonder in your presence,
  oblivious to your greatness and forgetful of your goodness.
Speak to us,
  as you spoke to Mary,
  and help us to catch a new sense of who you are,
  of all you have done,
  and of all you will yet do in our lives.
Help us to magnify your name,
  singing your praises and telling of your greatness,
  through Jesus Christ our Lord.
Amen.

34

Gracious God,
  you came to our world in fulfilment of your promises of old,
  your word embodied in a child lying in a manger.
You loved us so much that you staked everything
  to break down the barriers that keep us from you.
You shared our humanity from birth to death,
  so that with you we might share your eternity,
  life in all its fullness.
You became God with us,
  so that we might become one with *you*.
Teach us that, as you needed Mary's response then,
  you long for *our* response now:
  our willingness to accept your mercy
  and to experience the blessings you so long to give us.
Come again now and be born in our hearts,
  so that we may truly love you and joyfully serve you,
  this and every day,
  through Jesus Christ our Lord.
Amen.

35

Gracious God,
  we praise you for this season of Advent,
  this time for rejoicing and celebration,
  praise and worship,
  exulting in your goodness.
We praise you for coming in Christ,
  bringing in a new kingdom
  and anticipating an era of peace and justice
  when the poor will have plenty,
  the hungry be fed,
  and the lowly be lifted up.
We praise you that you want us to be a part of that,
  not just to share in it but also to play a part in bringing it to pass.
Forgive us that we sometimes lose sight of your purpose
  and underestimate your greatness.
Open our eyes to the breadth of your love,
  the wonder of your mercy and the extent of your goodness,
  and so may we give you the worship and adoration that is due to you,
  this and every day,
  through Jesus Christ our Lord.
Amen.

36
Loving God,
   the great festival of Christmas is drawing nearer
   and we are busy preparing for it –
   choosing presents,
   writing cards,
   planning get-togethers,
   buying food –
   so much that has become an accepted and expected part of this season.
Yet, in all the bustle, we so easily forget what matters most:
   responding to the gift of your Son.
Forgive us for relegating Jesus to the periphery of our celebrations
   rather than placing him at the centre where he belongs;
   for doing so much to prepare for Christmas on the surface
   yet so little to make ourselves ready within.
Open our hearts to welcome the living Christ into our lives,
   and so may we rejoice in his love,
   not just at Christmas,
   but always.
In his name we ask it.
Amen.

Christmas

37
Gracious God,
   help us to learn from the example of Mary.
Teach us this Christmastime
   to ponder, as she did, all that you have said and done:
   to listen again to familiar readings and carols,
   and to hear again the story we know so well,
   but also to consider what it all might mean;
   what you are saying not just to others but also to us.
Amid all the celebrations and rejoicing,
   help us to be still before you
   so that we may open our hearts to your living word,
   your renewing love
   and your redeeming power,
   and so know the presence of Jesus within us,
   by his grace.
Amen.

38
Gracious God,
   we praise you for the glorious message of this season:
   the glad tidings of great joy,
   ever old yet ever new.

We thank you for the faith of Mary,
   the commitment of Joseph,
   the message of the angels
   and the response of the shepherds –
   the way you changed their lives that day in Bethlehem.
Above all, though,
   we thank you that you have changed our lives too;
   that the good news these heard and responded to long ago
   is news still today –
   as special now as then,
   and for *us* as much as anyone!
Teach us never to forget that wonderful truth;
   never to overlook the fact that you have come to us in Christ.
May that knowledge burn brightly in our hearts,
   a constant source of joy and inspiration,
   whatever life may bring.
In the name of Christ, we ask it.
Amen.

39
Gracious God,
   we thank you for the joy of Christmastime:
   the joy you gave to Mary, shepherds and magi
   as you entered the world in Christ;
   the joy you have brought to generations across the centuries
   as they have come to faith;
   the joy you offer us now
   in a living and saving knowledge of Jesus Christ.
We praise you that, whatever we face, you are with us through him,
   supporting us by your love,
   enriching us by your grace,
   equipping us through your Spirit.
Inspire us afresh each day with the good news of Christ
   and the reality of his presence in our hearts,
   and so may we go on our way rejoicing,
   now and always.
Amen.

40
Gracious God,
   we thank you that you have given us good news in Christ,
   a message that has thrilled generations across the years,
   uplifting,
   encouraging,
   challenging
   and renewing.

We thank you for the way that message has spoken to us,
   shown to be glad tidings in so many ways.
Yet we confess that we sometimes lose our initial sense of awe and wonder,
   and no longer feel the urge to respond to your love
   as powerfully as we once did.
Forgive us for becoming casual and complacent in our faith,
   failing to make time to worship you,
   and forgetting the need to nurture our relationship with Jesus.
Speak to us again,
   meet us through the living Christ,
   and open our hearts to the renewing touch of your Holy Spirit.
So may we catch again the sense of urgency felt by the shepherds
   as they rushed to Bethlehem,
   and may the wonder of your love burn within us each day,
   to your glory.
Amen.

41
Living God,
   we remember today
   how shepherds responded to the message of the angels –
   how they hurried to Bethlehem
   and found the baby lying in a manger,
   and how afterwards they went on their way,
   sharing what they had seen and heard.
Teach us to share our experience of Christ in turn.
Help us to understand that your coming through him
   is good news for everyone,
   and that you want us to help make that known.
Enable us, then, to live each day with joy in our hearts
   and wonder in our eyes
   as we share the love you have shown us
   and make known the great thing you have done in Christ.
In his name we ask it.
Amen.

42
Lord Jesus Christ,
   we remember today how you came to our world
   and found no welcome;
   how,
   from the very beginning,
   you were shut out,
   no room for you even in the inn.
Forgive us that we are sometimes guilty of shutting you out in turn,
   failing to make room for you in so many areas of our lives.

Despite our words of faith and commitment,
　　we turn our back on you
　　when we would rather not face your challenge.
Forgive us,
　　and help us to make room for you,
　　not just this Christmas but always.
Teach us to give you not merely a token place in our hearts,
　　but to put you at the very centre of our lives.
Come now,
　　and make your home within us,
　　by your grace.
Amen.

43
Loving God,
　　remind us again that you are a God of grace,
　　reaching out to the bad as well as the good,
　　to sinners as well as saints.
Teach us that you chose Mary,
　　representative of the powerless;
　　shepherds,
　　examples of the socially marginalised;
　　and countless others across the years who society had rejected.
Help us, then, to turn to you,
　　acknowledging our faults and weaknesses,
　　knowing that, despite them all,
　　you have a place for us in your kingdom,
　　through Jesus Christ our Lord.
Amen.

44
Loving God,
　　we thank you for the great truth at the heart of this season –
　　your coming to our world in Christ.
We praise you that you go on coming,
　　day after day,
　　not just to others but also to us,
　　meeting and working within us through your Holy Spirit.
Forgive us everything that obstructs your coming –
　　all the trivia and irrelevancies with which we fill our lives
　　at the cost of time for you;
　　all the cares, doubts and unbelief
　　that prevent us sometimes from even glimpsing your presence.
Come afresh now,
　　and break through all the barriers in our lives,

so that we may know you more nearly by our side
and draw yet closer to you than we have ever been before.
Speak your word,
  grant your guidance,
  confer your power
  and fill us with your love,
  so that we may serve you as faithfully
  as you have served us in Christ.
In his name we ask it.
Amen.

45
Gracious God,
  you may not ask of us what you asked of Mary,
  but nonetheless your challenge comes to each one of us,
  calling us to avenues of service that we would never imagine possible.
Whoever we are,
  we all have a part to play in your purposes.
Grant us the humility we need to hear your voice
  and the faith we need to respond.
Like Mary,
  let each of us be ready to answer when you call:
  'I am the Lord's servant.
  Let it be to me just as you say.'
In Jesus' name we pray.
Amen.

46
Sovereign God,
  we can never repay your goodness
  and never fully express our thanks,
  but we bring you again today our praise and worship,
  offered in the name of Jesus.
Like the choir of angels on the night of his birth,
  we sing in adoration.
Like the shepherds,
  returning from the manger,
  we give you praise for everything we have experienced.
Like the magi,
  kneeling in wonder,
  we bring you our homage as a token of our love
  and a sign of our commitment.
All we think, say, do and are
  we bring to you in reverent praise and joyful celebration,
  in the name of Christ.
  Amen.

47

Loving God,
   we come today to remember with gratitude the birth of your Son.
We remember how prophets foretold his coming,
   and how those words were wonderfully fulfilled in Bethlehem.
We remember how you needed Mary to bring him into the world,
   and how she willingly allowed you to work through her.
We remember how shepherds heard the good news,
   and how, having seen the truth of it for themselves,
   they went on their way rejoicing.
We remember how Simeon held you in his arms,
   and with praise in his heart gave thanks to you.
We remember how generations since have seen your face revealed in Christ,
   and through him heard you speaking in a new way.
We remember the past
   so that we might discover you in the present,
   and find faith for the future.
Be born in our hearts today
   that we may be born again to eternal life.
Amen.

48

Loving God,
   you have come to us in Christ.
So now we come to you,
   to offer our worship,
   to hear your word
   and to reflect on your love.
Help us through all we share today
   to hear the story of Christmas speaking to us as though for the first time.
May familiar and well-loved words take on new meaning,
   so that we may share the elation of Mary,
   the excitement felt by the shepherds,
   and the wonder experienced by the wise men.
May what was news of great joy for them,
   bring joy likewise to us,
   this and every day,
   through Jesus Christ our Lord.
Amen.

First and Second Weeks after Christmas

49

Lord Jesus Christ,
   we remember today that those who first heard the good news
   were not the religious elite or those respected in the eyes of the world,

but shepherds –
ordinary, everyday people like each of us.
As so often during your ministry,
   you welcomed those whom society had little time for,
   who were counted as nothing;
   those who would have known their need
   and made no presumption on your goodness.
Teach us, through their experience,
   that, whoever we are,
   however insignificant we may feel,
   you value us for who we are,
   accept us despite our faults,
   and love us come what may.
May that knowledge be good news for us
   this and every day.
Amen.

50
Lord Jesus Christ,
   you were born so that you might die.
You took on our humanity
   so that you might experience also our mortality.
Only through identifying yourself so totally with us
   could you bridge the gap that separates us from God.
You showed us the way of love,
   and you followed it through to the end.
You proclaimed forgiveness,
   and you paid the price to make it possible.
In life and in death, you testified to the grace of the Father,
   and his purpose for all the world.
Help us, as we celebrate again your birth,
   never to forget that this was just the beginning of the story.
As we greet you now as the child of Bethlehem,
   so let us greet you also as the crucified Saviour
   and the risen Lord,
   and may we offer you,
   this and every day,
   our joyful worship
   in grateful praise.
Amen.

51
Loving God,
   challenge us through the example of the shepherds.
Teach us that it is not enough to accept the claims of the gospel
   on the basis of what someone else has said,

but that we need to experience the truth of it for ourselves.
Help us, then, to open our souls to the presence of Christ,
    and to welcome him into our lives.
Help us to know the reality of his Spirit at work within us,
    and to accept the message of the gospel,
        not just with our heads but also with our hearts.
In the name of Christ, we ask it.
Amen.

Epiphany

52

Lord Jesus Christ,
    like the wise men following your birth,
    teach us to search for you until we come to faith,
    and then to go on searching just as eagerly and whole-heartedly
    to discover more of your will and purpose for our lives.
Continue to surprise us with the wonder of your love
    and the awesomeness of your grace,
    and so may we know you and love you better each day,
    to the glory of your name.
Amen.

53

Lord Jesus Christ,
    you have told us to seek and we shall find.
Yet that search is not always easy.
As we look for meaning in our lives,
    there is so much that puzzles and perplexes.
The more we discover,
    the more we realise how little we have understood.
Give us the determination of the wise men to keep on looking,
    despite all that obscures you,
    until at last we find our perseverance rewarded
    and, glimpsing your glory,
    we kneel before you in joyful worship.
Amen.

54

Gracious God,
    such is your love for us that you go on calling
    however long it takes for us to respond,
    and you go on leading
    however tortuous our journey of faith may be.
We may put off a decision,
    keep you at arms length –

still you are there to guide,
striving to draw us to yourself.
We may encounter obstacles that impede our progress,
that lead us astray or that obscure the truth,
yet always you are there to set us back on the way.
Teach us that your love will never let us go,
and so help us to make our response
and to bring our lives to you in joyful homage,
knowing that you will continue to lead us until our journey's end,
through Jesus Christ our Lord.
Amen.

55
Sovereign God,
we are reminded today of the journey of the magi:
of how they stepped out into the unknown,
persevering despite adversity,
searching diligently until their quest was rewarded.
We come today, seeking in our turn:
looking to learn from their experience,
to worship the one before whom they knelt in homage,
to understand what his birth, life, death and resurrection mean for us.
Help us to discover each day a little more of your love,
and to discern more of your gracious purpose,
and so, in turn, may we offer you each moment a little more of our lives,
in joyful thanks
and glad thanksgiving
through Jesus Christ our Lord.
Amen.

Lent
see also Cost of Discipleship: Sacrifice and self-denial; Stillness and quiet
reflection; Temptation

56
Almighty and all-seeing God,
we thank you for this season of Lent:
a time to reflect upon our discipleship,
to consider our calling,
to examine ourselves
and to assess the health of our faith.
Help us to be honest in this:
to see ourselves as we really are
with all our weaknesses, ugliness and sinfulness.
Help us to face the things we usually prefer to push aside;
the unpleasant truths we sweep under the carpet,

pretending they are not there.
Help us to come to you now,
   acknowledging our faults,
   recognising our weaknesses
   and receiving your forgiveness,
   which alone can make us whole,
   through the grace of Christ.
Amen.

57

Gracious God,
   we thank you for the astonishing love you showed in Christ,
   sharing our humanity through him.
We praise you that you became flesh and blood like us,
   experiencing the same temptations we face,
   torn by the same fears,
   suffering the same pain
   and tasting the same joys and sorrows.
For the assurance this brings –
   the knowledge that you understand the worries, concerns,
   doubts and problems that confront us each day –
   receive our worship,
   in the name of Christ.
Amen.

58

Living God,
   forgive us that, too easily, we slip into a faith of negatives,
   imagining that you are more concerned with what we shouldn't do
   than with what we should.
Teach us that, although there is a very real place for self-denial,
   there is also a place for affirming and celebrating life in all its fullness.
Help us, then, to use this season of Lent as a time to grow and learn,
   to deepen our faith and strengthen our commitment;
   above all,
   a time to make more room for you,
   so that you can work in our lives
   and enrich our experience of your love,
   through Jesus Christ our Lord.
Amen.

59

Lord Jesus Christ,
   you faced temptation in the wilderness –
   enticement to put yourself first,
   to seek worldly glory,

to compromise your calling –
and steadfastly you refused.
You faced pressure throughout your ministry –
hostility,
ridicule,
threats,
rejection –
yet you carried on regardless,
true to your message,
true to your mission.
You faced the greatest test of all in Gethsemane,
as you wrestled there
with the prospect of betrayal, denial, suffering and death,
but once again you held firm,
putting God's will before your own.
What you said and what you did were always one,
each testifying to the other.
Lord Jesus Christ,
we fall so short of that goal,
words coming easily,
deeds to match rarely coming at all.
Forgive us,
and help us to show in our lives
the things we proclaim with our lips,
for your name's sake.
Amen.

60
Gracious God,
despite our resolve to serve you we are so easily led astray.
Like sheep,
we blindly follow the example of the crowd.
We congratulate ourselves on resisting the latest trend or fashion,
but the pressures to conform are more subtle than that,
often unseen,
unrecognised.
Help us to listen to *you* rather than the voices that surround us,
to stay close to *your* side and respond to *your* guidance.
And, should we find ourselves lost,
seek us out through Christ, the Good Shepherd,
and restore us to your fold,
for his name's sake.
Amen.

61

Lord Jesus Christ,
   sometimes you present us with a choice:
   between right and wrong,
   good and evil,
   life and death.
We know the way we ought to take,
   but we know also the cost,
   so we hold back,
   passing the buck instead to others.
Yet eventually we cannot evade your challenge,
   for in the very act of avoiding we make our decision.
Lord Jesus Christ,
   give us courage to face the choices life brings,
   and give us wisdom to choose the right way.
Amen.

62

Living God,
   it's easy to fool ourselves that we are observing Lent –
   giving up certain vices,
   denying ourselves particular pleasures,
   and making fine-sounding resolutions –
   but deep down we know that Lent should be more than this:
   a time rather for prayer and reflection,
   for self-examination and renewed commitment.
We come, then, seeking your will,
   your word,
   your guidance
   and your grace.
Nurture our feeble faith
   and help us to put you at the centre of this season,
   so that through it we may know you better,
   love you more fully
   and serve you more effectively,
   to the glory of your name.
Amen.

63

Loving God,
   you tell us that we will not be tested beyond our limits,
   that we shall not be tempted beyond what we can withstand.
But you tell us also to examine ourselves,
   to consider our faith,
   ensuring that we are serving and honouring you as we should be.

Forgive us that we all too easily grow casual in our discipleship,
  dismissing the need for such soul-searching.
Forgive us that we are content to meander along the way of discipleship,
  rather than dedicate ourselves single-mindedly to your service.
Help us to learn from the example of Jesus,
  and to remember that even he experienced a time of testing,
  and even he had to wrestle with temptation.
Give us grace, then, to be honest with ourselves
  and honest with you,
  and so to stand firm in faith
  whatever temptations we might face.
In Christ's name we ask it.
Amen.

Palm Sunday

64

Lord Jesus Christ,
  we are good at singing your praises when life goes as we want it to,
  but it's another matter when our expectations are overturned,
  our preconceptions challenged and our faith tested.
We are eager to receive your blessings
  but reluctant to take the way of sacrifice.
We are happy to proclaim you as king
  but hesitant in offering our service.
So often our commitment is short-lived,
  superficial and self-centred,
  more about our own well-being than your kingdom.
Forgive us,
  and, by your grace,
  help us to offer you true allegiance,
  whatever you may ask,
  to the glory of your name.
Amen.

65

Lord Jesus Christ,
  you entered Jerusalem on a wave of enthusiasm,
  greeted by your joyful people,
  by shouts of praise and protestations of loyalty on every side.
Yet you knew that the bubble would soon burst,
  that the welcome was only skin-deep.
We come today with equal gladness,
  but conscious that our commitment,
  like theirs,
  may not be as strong as it should be;

our faith fickle if put to the test,
our loyalty flawed.
Speak to us through the story of that first Palm Sunday,
and through the events that followed,
and so may our hosannas ring out as loudly tomorrow
as they do today.
In your name we ask it.
Amen.

66
Lord Jesus Christ,
no matter how often we hear it,
how often we picture it,
we can barely begin to imagine what you went through on the cross.
We know you suffered,
we know you died,
but we cannot comprehend the agony you experienced,
or the terrible sense of isolation you must have endured
as the life ebbed from you.
We cannot imagine it,
but we need to try,
for only then can we recognise how much you loved us.
So we come today,
to listen again to words of Scripture,
to sing again well-loved hymns,
and to offer you our prayers,
our time,
our money
and our worship.
Receive all we bring,
and speak to us afresh of the immensity of your love
and the awesomeness of your grace,
for we ask it in your name.
Amen.

67
Lord Jesus Christ,
we are reminded of how you entered Jerusalem
to shouts of joy and celebration.
But we remember too how quickly that welcome evaporated,
how soon the mood of the crowd changed.
Lord Jesus Christ,
we know all too well that we are not so different,
our commitment to you so often short-lived,
superficial,
self-centred.

Help us to welcome you into our lives with true gladness,
  and to go on serving you come what may,
  now and always.
Amen.

Holy Week

68

Loving God,
  through your Son you walked the way of the cross,
  each step leading you inexorably to suffering, humiliation and death.
We know it,
  and yet we continue to marvel,
  for such love defies human logic,
  transcending anything we can give in return.
Open our hearts afresh to the wonder of your love,
  and help us to glimpse more fully all it cost you
  and all it offers to us.
So help us to respond,
  with grateful hearts
  in joyful service,
  to the glory of your name.
Amen.

69

Lord Jesus Christ,
  you didn't take the *easy* way as we would have done:
  the path of popular acclaim,
  of least resistance.
You took the *right* way:
  the way of truth, love and service,
  and you followed it faithfully,
  knowingly,
  undeterred by the consequences,
  intent on serving others rather than yourself.
Forgive us that we are so easily led astray,
  thoughts so much for ourselves and so little for you.
Forgive us for our willingness to compromise,
  even when we know the way we ought to take.
Strengthen our resolve,
  increase our faith,
  and help us to stay true to our calling and true to you,
  to the glory of your name.
Amen.

70

Lord Jesus Christ,
  you gave so much;
  forgive us that we give so little.
You refused to count the cost;
  we resent even the smallest sacrifice being asked of us.
You took the way of others;
  we take the way of self.
Lord Jesus,
  all good, all loving,
  we have no claim on your goodness,
  no reason to expect your mercy,
  yet, despite that, still you died for us.
Have mercy, we pray,
  and, poor though it may be, accept the discipleship we offer,
  and use us in the service of your kingdom,
  to the glory of your name.
Amen.

71

Lord Jesus Christ,
  as we remember your triumphant entry into Jerusalem,
  we are reminded of how easy it would have been
  for you to take the easy option,
  to follow the way of the world.
With the shouts of welcome still ringing in your ears,
  the hosannas of the crowd still fresh in your memory,
  it must have been so tempting to give them what they wanted,
  to be the sort of Messiah they hoped you would be.
But with you there was no compromise,
  no watering down of your message for the sake of popular acclaim.
You stayed true to your calling despite the inevitable consequences.
Lord,
  we find it so hard to stay true in turn,
  so difficult not to bend a little here
  and give a little there.
Give us courage to walk the way of discipleship,
  and, by your grace, to stay true to you
  come what may.
In your name we pray.
Amen.

72

Lord Jesus Christ,
  we come again in this Holy Week
  to reflect on your journey to the cross.

You knew where that journey was leading right from the very start,
    and you did your best to ensure that your disciples understood too.
Yet they either couldn't believe, or wouldn't believe,
    what you were telling them.
Forgive us that all too often we refuse to accept
    what we don't want to hear.
Forgive us that we prefer to focus on the rewards of discipleship
    rather than the cost.
Help us now, as we worship you,
    to learn from your determination to complete the course
    and, in turn, to run faithfully the race set before us,
    looking to you,
    the pioneer and perfecter of our faith,
    in whose name we pray.
Amen.

73
Lord Jesus Christ,
    you were under no illusions about those you called to follow you.
You knew that Judas would betray you,
    Peter deny you,
    and the rest of the Apostles forsake you,
    yet still you continued on your way to the cross.
We marvel at your amazing grace that goes beyond our understanding.
Help us as we recall the stories of Judas and Peter today
    to appreciate the wonder of your love for us who deserve it so little,
    and in return to love you who deserves it so much.
In your name we ask it.
Amen.

Maundy Thursday

74
'If it is possible, take this cup from me.'
Lord Jesus,
    we remember that desperate cry of yours
    in the darkness of Gethsemane;
    that cry of anguish as you faced up to the horror of the cross.
We remember that, knowing full well what the future held,
    you were still able to say, 'Not my will, O God, but yours',
    and you did so, not because you are different
    but because you are fully one with us,
    sharing our humanity,
    ready, out of love, to offer your all
    so that we might taste life in all its fullness.

Lord,
    help us to recall everything you went through for our sakes,
    and to appreciate the magnitude of what you did.
Teach us how much you loved us,
    and so may we offer our love in return,
    to you and to all,
    for your name's sake.
Amen.

75

Lord Jesus Christ,
    you broke bread with your disciples
    you shared wine,
    and you told them to go on doing likewise in memory of you.
For countless years,
    across countless generations,
    your people have done just that.
And so now we come,
    to share in your supper,
    and to remember.
This night of all nights reminds us of the great truths of the gospel –
    of who you were,
    what you did,
    why you came,
    and when you shall come again.
Help us, as we recall everything you went through in Gethsemane,
    and all that went after,
    to remember you did it for us as much as any.
To you be all praise and glory,
    now and for evermore.
Amen.

76

Lord Jesus Christ,
    we have broken bread,
    we have shared wine –
    and we have done it,
    together with your people across the centuries,
    in remembrance of you.
You promise that the time will come
    when we share with you in your Father's kingdom,
    a time when your will shall be done
    and all things shall be made new.
Until then, may the memory of all you have done shape our lives
    and guide our footsteps,
    to the glory of your name.
Amen.

77

Lord Jesus Christ,
   you command us to eat and drink in remembrance of you,
   and so we come now, recalling again the wonder of your love.
We remember how you shared bread and wine with your followers,
   knowing that they would fail you.
We remember how in Gethsemane
   you faced the awful and awesome prospect of the cross,
   alone.
We remember how you faced arrest, interrogation and brutality
   with humility.
We remember your quiet acceptance of human hatred and evil
   directed against you who knew no hatred and had done no evil.
We remember your willingness to embrace suffering and death
   so that we might find healing, wholeness and new life.
Lord Jesus Christ,
   we remember your great love,
   and we marvel at how much you were willing to bear for our sakes.
Amen.

78

Lord Jesus Christ,
   we hear so much as Christians about joy and celebration
   that we can feel sometimes it is wrong to feel anything else.
Yet in Gethsemane you knew the pain of sorrow;
   the agony of betrayal,
   denial and rejection.
You experienced life at its darkest and found it hard to bear.
May that truth give us strength in times of need –
   the ability to face grief openly and honestly,
   knowing that you have been there before us
   and that you understand all we are going through.
Amen.

79

Lord Jesus Christ,
   we know the story of your death and resurrection so well
   that we can forget sometimes what it actually involved,
   overlooking the fact that you were human just as we are,
   experiencing the same sorrow, uncertainty,
   pain and fear
   that any of us would have experienced in your place.
You struggled there at Gethsemane with anguish of spirit
   as you looked to the future,
   striving to see beyond the cross but seeing only the agony of death,

yet you continued on your chosen path,
   faithful to the last.
Lord Jesus Christ,
   help us to realise the extent of your love,
   and to offer at least a little of ours in return.
Amen.

80

Lord Jesus Christ,
   you spoke about loving our enemies,
   praying for those who persecute us,
   turning the other cheek,
   and there in Gethsemane you showed that you meant those words,
   no matter what the cost.
Lord,
   we are good at saying the right things,
   but all too often it is merely talk,
   found wanting when the real test comes.
Help us,
   like you,
   to practise what we preach.
Amen.

81

Lord Jesus Christ,
   we remember today the hours of testing you endured in Gethsemane:
   the heartbreak you felt,
   the fear you experienced,
   the questions you wrestled with and the uncertainty you faced.
We remember that, despite it all, you stood firm,
   refusing to be swayed from your calling.
We remember how you went on to endure the agony of the cross
   and the darkness of death.
So now we come,
   able to look forward in faith,
   anticipating that time when we will share with you
   in your Father's kingdom;
   a time when there will be an end to sorrow and suffering,
   sin and death.
Save us from ever losing sight of that destiny.
We look back,
   we look forward,
   and thus we commit ourselves in confidence
   to your service here and now,
   knowing that you are the same Lord,

yesterday, today and tomorrow –
the one in whom we can safely put our trust.
Amen.

Good Friday

82
Lord Jesus Christ,
    forgive us that, living as we do in the light of Easter,
    we lose sight sometimes of the darkness of Good Friday,
Remind us today that for those who saw the life slip from you
    as you hung on the cross,
    there could be no mistaking the truth,
    no escaping the awfulness of the moment.
You endured the pain of betrayal,
    the hurt of denial,
    the humiliation of mockery
    and, finally, the awful isolation of separation from your Father
    as you took our sins on your shoulders –
    and you did it for such as us.
Lord Jesus,
    we marvel at your love;
    at the fact that you were willing to go not just part of the way
    but the whole way
    to redeem the world.
We marvel that you,
    in whom is life eternal,
    were willing to experience death
    so that we might taste that life.
Teach us today to appreciate the wonder of that sacrifice
    and to recognise all that it continues to mean in so many ways.
Amen.

83
Lord Jesus Christ,
    we marvel again today at your astonishing love:
    the way you endured the humiliation of Gethsemane,
    the agony of the cross
    and the darkness of the tomb,
    not because you *had* to
    but because you *chose* to.
We praise you that, despite the jeers and ridicule you faced,
    your concern was always for others rather than yourself,
    and thus you freely chose the way of humility, service and self-sacrifice:
    the lonely path of the cross.

Above all,
    we praise you for your faithfulness to the last –
    that though you could so easily have stepped down from the cross,
    you didn't;
    and though you could have saved yourself,
    you preferred instead to save the world.
Lord Jesus Christ,
    however often we hear it,
    still we are amazed by the magnitude of your love
    and the awesomeness of your sacrifice.
Receive our praise and accept our worship,
    for your name's sake.
Amen.

84

Living God,
    in so many ways this is the blackest of days
    recalling the darkest of moments:
    a day on which hearts were broken
    and faith tested to the limit,
    a day of appalling suffering
    and agonising death,
    a day when all hell was let loose
    and love seemed overwhelmed.
Yet we can call this day 'Good Friday',
    for in all of that horror you were there.
In the despair,
    pain,
    humiliation
    and sorrow,
    you were supremely at work,
    demonstrating the immensity of your love.
Living God,
    as we recall those terrible yet wonderful events,
    give us new insight into what you did that day,
    for us and for all,
    through Jesus Christ our Lord.
Amen.

85

Lord Jesus Christ,
    whoever we are,
    whatever we have done,
    we know it is never too late to respond to your love,
    for you are always ready to forgive and forget,
    always waiting to pick up the pieces of our lives and help us start again.

We praise you that this is why you came –
    to offer a clean break to everyone who recognises their need;
    a new beginning in this life and the life to come –
    and, in that assurance, we come now seeking your help and mercy,
    for our sin and weakness is ever before us.
Lord Jesus Christ,
    as the thief asked on the cross, so we ask too:
    'When you come into your kingdom,
    remember me.'
Amen.

86
Lord Jesus Christ,
    you suffered so much for our sakes –
    pain of mind as well as body:
    the pain of waiting for the end,
    of mockery and rejection,
    of betrayal, denial and misunderstanding,
    of flogging and physical blows,
    of thorns pressed on to your head
    and nails driven into your hands and feet,
    of hanging in agony on that cross.
Lord Jesus Christ,
    as we celebrate all you have given us,
    help us never to forget what it cost you.
Amen.

87
Lord Jesus Christ,
    there are many who suffer,
    many who endure untold agony of body, mind and spirit,
    but few would do so willingly,
    and fewer still choose that course as their vocation in life.
Yet you came and walked the way of the cross
    with single-minded determination,
    and you gave your life freely
    so that one day there will be an end to all suffering and sorrow;
    a time when all will rejoice in the wonder of your love
    and experience the joy of your kingdom.
Until then, Lord, reach out into our world of darkness,
    into every place of need,
    and bring the comfort, strength, peace and hope that you alone can bring,
In your name we ask it.
Amen.

Easter

see also New beginnings: Resurrection hope

88

Gracious God,
   we thank you that our faith is not founded on theory or speculation –
   on the ideas of theologians or the musings of philosophers.
It is rooted in what individuals have seen and heard,
   in the living testimony of ordinary people like us,
   in the testimony of countless generations of believers
   who have encountered the risen Christ for themselves through his Spirit.
In him,
   you came,
   you lived,
   you died,
   you rose again,
   making yourself known through the concrete events of history.
For all who saw for themselves and passed the message on,
   receive our thanks.
And for all that we experience today of your continuing love
   and your life-giving purpose,
   we give you our praise in joyful worship,
   through Jesus Christ,
   our risen, victorious Saviour.
Amen.

89

Lord Jesus Christ,
   like the two disciples on the Emmaus Road,
   so often we journey through life unaware of your presence.
Though we talk of your resurrection
   it does not stir our hearts or capture our imagination
   in the way it should.
Yet even though we may not realise it,
   you are there with us,
   matching your stride to ours,
   waiting to meet us along the way.
Open our eyes
   that we may see and know you better.
Amen.

90

Lord Jesus Christ,
   it was not just you who was broken that day you hung on a cross –
   it was your disciples too,
   their hearts broken just as surely,

their dreams and hopes snuffed out,
   their faith cut from beneath them and laid to rest.
It was not just you who rose again that day you emerged from the tomb –
   it was your disciples too,
   their hearts beating once more with joyful anticipation,
   their vision for the future reborn,
   their faith rekindled, bursting into unquenchable flame.
Come to us now where we are broken –
   where love had died,
   where hope has faded,
   where faith has grown cold.
Reach out and touch us in body, mind and spirit,
   and help us to walk in the newness of life
   which you alone can bring.
In your name we ask it.
Amen.

91
Lord Jesus Christ,
   we rejoice today in the good news of your resurrection.
You met with Mary in the garden,
   bringing laughter after tears.
You met with women returning from the tomb,
   bringing confidence after confusion.
You met with Cleopas on the Emmaus Road,
   bringing hope after dismay.
You met with the Apostles in a room barred against the world,
   bringing joy after sorrow.
You met with Thomas, in his disbelief,
   bringing faith after doubt.
You met with Paul on his way to Damascus,
   bringing love after hatred.
You met with countless generations across the centuries,
   bringing renewal after rejection.
Meet with us now, in this day, this moment,
   bringing light after darkness.
Fill our hearts with the new life of Easter,
   until that day when, with all your people,
   we enter your kingdom
   and rejoice in the wonder of your love for all eternity.
In your name we pray.
Amen.

92
Sovereign God,
   we don't understand how you raised Jesus from the dead –
   how you breathed life into his broken body,
   how you rolled the stone away from the tomb,
   how he somehow appeared unrecognised to Mary in the garden
   and to disciples on the Emmaus Road;
   how he walked through locked doors to be with the Apostles;
   how he repeatedly appeared from nowhere to stand among his followers.
What we *do* understand is this:
   that he changed the lives of all who met him,
   turning their sorrow into celebration,
   their despair into hope
   and their doubt into faith;
   and that he is with us now through his life-giving Spirit,
   remaking our lives in turn,
   giving us joy, peace and a sense of purpose
   such as we never imagined possible before.
We do not understand,
   but we believe,
   we rejoice
   and we offer you our grateful worship
   in the name of that same Jesus,
   our risen Lord and Saviour.
Amen.

93
Living God,
   we praise you for the great truth of Easter –
   the message that your love will not be defeated.
When human evil had done its worst,
   despite every effort to frustrate your purpose,
   still your will triumphed!
The stone was rolled away,
   the tomb was empty,
   Christ had risen!
May that truth fire us each day with new hope,
   new confidence,
   and new enthusiasm,
   knowing that whatever obstacles we may face
   and whatever may fight against us,
   there is nothing that will finally be able to thwart your purpose
   or to deny your saving purpose,
   in Jesus Christ our Lord.
Amen.

94

Lord Jesus Christ,
   we praise you that we can worship you
   not simply as the crucified Christ
   but as our risen Lord and Saviour.
We praise you that death was not the end but a new beginning,
   not simply for you but for us!
We praise you for this time of joy, thanksgiving and rejoicing,
   a time that speaks of victory, renewal and hope.
For the great message of Easter
   that has spoken to countless people across the years
   and that continues to speak to us today,
   receive our joyful and grateful worship.
Come among us now, in your risen power,
   and send us out to proclaim your name
   and live to your glory,
   for your name's sake.
Amen.

95

Lord Jesus Christ,
   you appeared to different people
   at different places
   at different times:
   to Mary in the garden,
   to Cleopas and his companion on the Emmaus Road,
   to the disciples in the upper room,
   to your followers in Galilee.
Each had their own unique encounter with you,
   and it was only when you met with them,
   face to face,
   that the truth dawned;
   only then that they dared to believe you were alive.
Lord Jesus Christ,
   we cannot see you quite as they did,
   but we too can meet with you
   and experience the reality of your living presence.
Meet with us now, as we worship you.
Live in us always
   so that our lives might redound to your praise and glory.
Amen.

96

Living God,
   we praise you for the wonder of Easter –
   this day that changed the world for ever!

We rejoice in the victory of Christ:
    his triumph over evil,
    hatred,
    despair,
    and even death itself.
Living God,
    we praise you for the victory you have won,
    and for the assurance it brings that nothing in life or death
    can ever separate us from your love;
    nothing in heaven or earth defeat your loving purpose for all the world.
To you be praise and glory,
    this day and always.
Amen.

97
Living God,
    we praise you once more for the good news of Easter,
    the triumphant message of resurrection –
    new hope,
    new joy,
    new life!
We praise you for the truth at its heart:
    that your love could not be kept down,
    your purpose could not be defeated
    and your mercy could not be destroyed.
Teach us that what was true then is true now –
    that nothing can stand in the way
    of your sovereign power and redeeming grace.
Assure us, then,
    even when faith seems to fly in the face of reason,
    to trust in you,
    confident that your will shall be done
    and your kingdom come,
    through Jesus Christ our Lord.
Amen.

98
Lord Jesus Christ,
    we thank you for the great message of Easter –
    that in what the world counted defeat you won the greatest of victories.
We praise you for your triumph over evil and death,
    and for everything this has meant over the years to so many people.
Most of all,
    we thank you for our own experiences of your resurrection power –
    the times you have brought us victory
    over all that stops us living life to the full.

Teach us to live each day in the light of what you have done,
    confident that no situation,
    however dreadful it may seem,
    is finally beyond your power to redeem,
    and so may we put our trust in you always,
    for this life
    and the life to come.
Amen.

99
Sovereign God,
    sometimes it seems too good to be true –
    the cross,
    the empty tomb
    and the promise of new life for all eternity.
There are times when,
    for all our faith,
    we struggle to accept it,
    not because we don't want to
    but because we want to so much,
    and we wonder whether we are fooling ourselves,
    telling ourselves what we want to believe.
Yet you remind us today that this is precisely how the Apostles felt
    until they met with the risen Christ
    and knew the truth for themselves,
    not as speculation
    but as an indisputable experience.
Rekindle our faith this Easter time.
Assure us,
    through experiencing again
    the presence of the risen Christ within our hearts,
    that with you nothing is too good to be true,
    for you are able to do more than anyone could ever imagine.
To you be praise and glory,
    now and for evermore.
Amen.

100
Sovereign God,
    we praise you today for the power of the gospel;
    the way across the centuries it has spoken to so many lives.
We praise you for everything you achieved in Christ,
    transforming not just individuals but the very course of history
    through his life, death and resurrection.
We praise you that you involved yourself in human history,

not standing aloof from our need
but sharing our humanity so that we might share your eternity.
For your life-giving grace that continues to reach out into the world
and for your mighty strength that will never rest
until your will is done and your kingdom come,
receive our glad and joyful worship,
in the name of Christ.
Amen.

101
Lord Jesus Christ,
we celebrate again today your triumph over falsehood and evil;
the fact that all the attempts to discredit you
and to suppress the truth of your resurrection
came to nothing,
for it was impossible to deny the reality of your presence
in the hearts of those who knew you.
Forgive us that we are not always as truthful as we should be,
slipping so easily into white lies,
or hiding behind half-truths.
Remind us that your truth can set us free,
and so teach us to receive it with joy,
speak it in love and live by it in faith,
trusting in your love that alone will never fail.
In your name we ask it.
Amen.

102
Lord Jesus Christ,
you brought new beginnings out of what had seemed the end;
new hope in what had seemed hopeless;
new purpose in what had seemed to deny all meaning.
We celebrate that truth,
yet we confess how hard we find it sometimes
to believe that such new beginnings can apply to us;
that we too can start again.
We look at our own situation –
the opportunities missed,
hopes dashed,
possibilities denied,
and dreams extinguished –
and we see no prospect of life rising fresh from the ashes.
Yet, as you came to Mary, the Apostles and countless others since,
so you come now afresh today in your life-giving, renewing power.
Teach us,
however hopeless circumstances might seem,

however much we may feel ourselves to be at a dead end,
    never to lose our sense of all that you are able to do.
Remind us that endings can lead to new beginnings,
    that new life can spring from the old,
    and so may we look forward with confidence
    to everything you will yet do in our lives.
In your name we ask it.
Amen.

103
Living God,
    we look at the world and at our lives
    and we are dismayed sometimes at how little seems to change.
We go on making the same mistakes we've always made,
    and all around us there seems to be as much sorrow, suffering,
    hatred and evil as there has ever been.
Help us to hold on to the conviction that things can change;
    to remember how,
    in the resurrection of Christ,
    you overcame the power of sin and death.
Help us to remember that
    though everything may seem to conspire against you,
    you have won the victory through him –
    a victory that nothing can ever undo –
    and so may we trust in your ability to transform and renew all things,
    by his grace.
Amen.

Sundays after Easter

104
Sovereign God,
    we thank you that Easter is not just about events long ago
    but about now;
    not just about others
    but about us;
    not just about certain aspects of life
    but about life itself!
We thank you for the truths of Easter we can continue to celebrate today:
    the victory of good over evil,
    love over hate,
    and life over death;
    the turning of weakness into strength,
    fear into courage,
    and doubt into faith;

a new beginning where it had seemed like the end,
hope where there had been despair;
and confidence where there had been confusion.
Help us to live each day in the light of Easter,
   with its joy bubbling up in our hearts,
   its laughter shining from our eyes,
   and its message always on our lips.
So may others,
   seeing the difference it has made to us,
   discover the difference it can make for them,
   through Jesus Christ our Lord.
Amen.

105

Living God,
   your ways are not our ways,
   neither are your thoughts our thoughts.
There is so much in our lives that troubles and confuses us,
   so much hurt and pain that we cannot begin to make sense of.
Yet we know that in Jesus you have shared our humanity,
   experiencing not just the good but the bad.
You understand what it means to be hurt,
   to endure suffering,
   to face even death itself.
As well as our joys you have shared our sorrows.
Living God,
   we thank you for the assurance this gives us:
   that whatever we face you will be with us in it.
Teach us to live each day in the light of that truth,
   and so to live always as your Easter people,
   to the glory of your name.
Amen.

106

Lord Jesus Christ,
   we thank you that you meet us day by day,
   just as you met your disciples in the days following your resurrection.
We thank you that your victory of good over evil,
   love over hate
   and life over death
   continues to make such a difference to our lives,
   just as it did to theirs,
   bringing new beginnings when it seems like the end,
   new hope where there seems only despair.
For turning weakness into strength,

fear into confidence
and doubt into faith,
receive our praise
and continue to work that miracle in our lives and our world today,
making all things new,
to the glory of your name.
Amen.

Ascension Day

107
Lord Jesus Christ,
   we praise you today for the wonder of your mercy,
   the extent of your love and your great gift of life.
We rejoice that you came into our world
   not just to be an earthly Messiah but a universal Saviour,
   the King of kings and Lord of lords.
We thank you not only for everything you have done
   but for everything you have yet to do –
   the blessings we have yet to experience,
   the insights we have yet to discover,
   and the joys you yet hold in store.
Remind us each day that you are able not simply to meet our needs
   but also to give us far more than we can ever ask or imagine.
So may we look forward in hope,
   and live each day with joy in the light of your love.
Amen.

108
Lord Jesus Christ,
   teach us what it means to acknowledge you as Lord.
Help us to offer you the worship you deserve:
   to bring you our praise and homage,
   and to acknowledge you as King of kings and Lord of lords.
But help us also to offer you the service you deserve:
   to respond to everything you have done for us
   through working wholeheartedly for your kingdom,
   committing ourselves body, mind and soul
   to the fulfilment of your purpose
   and the making known of your love.
Take us,
   and use us as you will,
   for your glory.
Amen.

109

Lord Jesus Christ,
  we claim to follow you,
  and we declare you to be the Lord and King of our lives,
  but all too often our actions deny our words.
We have broken your commandments,
  betrayed your love
  and ignored your guidance –
  our faith fickle
  and our allegiance poor.
Forgive us all the ways we fail you,
  through thought, word and deed.
Forgive us our limited understanding of your greatness
  and the narrowness of our vision.
Forgive our inability to grasp the values of your kingdom,
  still less to base our lives upon them.
Lord Jesus,
  we come before your throne,
  throwing ourselves upon your grace,
  and asking you to receive our homage and service,
  poor though these may be.
Rule in our hearts and use us for the growth of your kingdom,
  to the glory of your name.
Amen.

110

Lord Jesus Christ,
  you were brought low,
  yet you have been lifted high.
You were the servant of all,
  yet you are above all and beyond all.
You were despised and rejected,
  yet your name is exalted above all names.
You were fully human,
  yet you are divine.
You were taken into heaven,
  yet you are here by our sides.
You are higher than our highest thoughts,
  yet we can know you as a friend.
So, with all your people in every age,
  we bow before you and confess you as our risen Saviour,
  the King of kings and Lord of lords,
  to the glory of God the Father.
Amen.

111

Living God,
  as we remember today how Jesus departed into heaven,
  we remember your promise that he will one day return in glory.
We look back to his mysterious Ascension long ago,
  we look forward to that time when he will come again,
  and we ask you to help us understand what all that has to say to us
  here and now.
Open our ears.
Open our eyes.
Open our minds.
Open our hearts.
May all we share in today
  give us a deeper insight into all you have done for us in Christ,
  and a greater sense of all you have yet to do.
In his name we ask it.
Amen.

112

Baby of Bethlehem, born in a stable,
  we worship you.
Child of Nazareth, full of grace and truth,
  we acknowledge you.
Man of Galilee, teacher, preacher, healer, redeemer,
  we praise you.
Son of David, coming in humility to claim your kingdom,
  we greet you.
Suffering servant, bruised, beaten, broken,
  we salute you.
Lord of the empty tomb, risen and triumphant,
  we honour you.
King of kings, exalted by the side of the Father,
  we adore you.
Jesus Christ, our Lord and Saviour,
  receive the homage we offer,
  to the glory of your name.
Amen.

113

Jesus of Bethlehem,
  be born in us today.
Jesus of Galilee,
  touch our lives with your presence.
Jesus of Gethsemane,
  strengthen us in times of trial.

Jesus of Calvary,
    have mercy upon us, for we do not know what we do.
Jesus of the empty tomb,
    lead us from light into darkness, from death into life.
Jesus of eternity,
    the Word made flesh,
    the King of kings and Lord of lords,
    walk with us until our journey's end,
    and to you be glory this day and for evermore.
Amen.

114

Lord Jesus Christ,
    we are good at singing your praises
    when life is going according to plan,
    but when our expectations are overturned,
    our preconceptions challenged
    and our faith tested to the limit
    it is another matter.
We are quick then to complain,
    to question your purpose,
    even to forget you altogether.
We proclaim your sovereignty when it suits us,
    but reject your authority when it doesn't.
Teach us to be faithful in the good times and the bad,
    giving you honour in whatever we may face
    and confessing you,
    through word and deed,
    as King of kings and Lord of lords,
    to the glory of your name.
Amen.

115

Lord Jesus Christ,
    you are greater than we can ever imagine,
    before all,
    beyond all,
    in all
    and over all.
Forgive us for losing sight of your greatness;
    for underestimating the breadth of your love
    and the extent of your purpose;
    for tying you down to the things of earth
    rather than opening our hearts to the kingdom of heaven.

Broaden our vision,
   enlarge our understanding,
   deepen our faith,
   kindle our imagination,
   that we may glimpse your glory,
   and work more faithfully for your kingdom.
In your name we ask it.
Amen.

116
Lord Jesus Christ,
   we greet you as King of kings and Lord of lords.
We acknowledge your greatness,
   we recognise your authority,
   we celebrate your exaltation,
   we commit ourselves to your kingdom.
Open our eyes, this day, to the wonder of your Ascension
   and all it means for our lives.
Stir our imagination
   increase our commitment,
   widen our perspectives,
   strengthen our faith.
Equip us for all you would have us do,
   and so may we live to your glory,
   now and always.
Amen.

Pentecost

117
Living God,
   we remember today how you transformed the lives of the Apostles:
   how, through the breath of your Spirit,
   you turned their fear into confidence,
   their weakness into strength,
   their doubt into faith,
   and their sorrow into joy.
Come to us now, through that same Spirit.
Take our weak and hesitant faith
   and fill us with unshakeable trust in your purpose.
Take our stumbling discipleship,
   and grant us energy and enthusiasm to proclaim the gospel
   through word and deed.
Take our fear and anxieties,
   and give us courage
   and your peace that passes understanding.

Take our gifts and talents,
 and use them in the service of your kingdom.
Living God,
 help us to remember today not simply all you did *once*,
 but to rejoice in all you are doing *now*
 and all you shall continue to do through your Holy Spirit.
In the name of Christ we ask it.
Amen.

118

Lord Jesus Christ,
 you told the disciples to expect the gift of the Holy Spirit,
 yet when it came it took them by surprise,
 bursting into their lives in a way beyond all their expectations.
Suddenly life was transformed for them,
 full of untold possibilities.
You tell us also to expect the gift of the Spirit,
 yet we too are taken by surprise.
You want to transform our lives
 to open the door to new horizons,
 but we close our hearts or tie you down to our own expectations.
Lord Jesus,
 as we remember today that day of Pentecost long ago,
 help us to open our lives to the movement of your Spirit now,
 for your name's sake.
Amen.

119

Living God,
 we tend automatically to associate the gift of the Spirit
 with the day of Pentecost –
 that incredible day
 when you turned the lives of the Apostles upside down,
 that day which in many ways marked the birth of the Christian Church.
Yet wonderful as that day was,
 your word reminds us that it is only part of the story,
 for it speaks also of less dramatic but equally real gifts of your Spirit:
 encouraging,
 enabling,
 serving,
 supporting –
 all manner of gifts that, though they do not hit the headlines,
 contribute powerfully to the growth of your kingdom.
Help us to recognise today the way you come to us,
 the gifts you have given
 and how you would have us use these in your service.

Teach us to open our lives to your Spirit's movement
  and so may we be equipped to love and serve you better,
  to the glory of your name.
Amen.

120
Gracious God,
  we thank you that we can know you for ourselves
  through the living presence of your Holy Spirit.
We praise you that, by your Spirit, you meet our innermost needs,
  filling our souls to overflowing with joy,
  peace,
  hope
  and power.
We celebrate the way you are always moving in our lives,
  deepening our faith,
  enriching our experience,
  strengthening our commitment
  and enlarging our vision.
Help us to open our lives more fully to the presence of your Spirit,
  so that we may know you better
  and be equipped to serve you more fully,
  to the glory of your name.
Amen.

121
Lord Jesus Christ,
  we know what fruits you would like to see in our lives:
  love,
  joy,
  peace,
  patience,
  kindness,
  generosity,
  faithfulness,
  gentleness
  and self-control.
We know we ought to show these,
  but we know also how rarely we do,
  how all too often the fruits we yield are so very different.
Instead of living by the Spirit we live by the flesh,
  and the results are plain for all to see.
Forgive us,
  and by your grace grant us another chance to start again.
Put your Spirit within us

and nurture our faith,
so that the time will come when our lives will bear a rich harvest
to the glory of your name.
Amen.

Trinity Sunday

122
Eternal God,
you are greatest than our highest thoughts,
defying full expression
and ultimately beyond our limited understanding,
yet through Jesus you have given us a glimpse of your glory.
We recall how he spoke of you as Father,
not just his but ours –
a Father watching over us from on high.
We remember how he spoke to you as a friend,
there beside him as you are with us,
by our sides through thick and thin.
We rejoice that he faithfully followed the prompting of your Spirit,
opening the way to experience your living presence,
vitally real within us,
deepening our faith and enriching our lives.
Eternal God,
help us to recognise that to see Jesus is to see you,
that to receive his Spirit is to know your power,
that to respond to his call is to be touched by your love,
for you are Three in One and One in Three.
Open our hearts to your awesome presence
and to all the ways you reveal your grace,
so that we may honour you this day and always
as Father, Son and Holy Spirit.
Amen.

123
Almighty and everlasting God,
we are here before you.
Grant us a glimpse of your awesome presence,
and help us to worship you with reverent praise.
Father God,
we are here before you.
Grant us a sense of your everlasting arms encircling us,
and help us to trust always in your loving purpose.
Lord Jesus Christ,
we are here before you.

Grant us grace to hear your call,
    and help us to follow in your footsteps
    wherever that might lead.
Holy Spirit,
    we are here before you.
Grant us openness of heart, mind and spirit,
    and help us to know your peace and power.
Almighty and everlasting God,
    Father, Son and Holy Spirit,
    we are here before you.
Grant that we may know you better,
    and help us to live and work for you, this day and always.
Amen.

124
Gracious God,
    there are some experiences that we cannot put into words,
    however hard we try –
    moments of joy, love, awe, hope, thanksgiving, celebration
    and so many more.
Yet though these may defy expression,
    we know they are as real and special as any.
So it is with our experience of you.
Together with your Church across the ages
    we strive to articulate our faith,
    to describe somehow everything that you mean to us –
    your awesome sovereignty,
    your unfailing care,
    your intimate closeness,
    your presence within.
Yet the language we use –
    Father, Son and Holy Spirit,
    Three in One and One in Three –
    seems hopelessly inadequate.
It makes no sense according to human logic,
    yet we know it to be true,
    not in our minds but in our hearts.
So we rejoice,
    and acknowledge you as our God
    in joyful worship
    and grateful praise,
    one God,
    world without end.
  Amen.

125

Mighty God,
  beyond all space and time,
  greater than our minds can fully grasp,
  ruler over all that is and has been and shall be,
  we worship you.
We worship you as the God made known to us in Christ –
  a God all good and wholly other,
  and yet a God who loves us as a father loves his children.
We worship you as the God we experience within us –
  the God who fires our imagination
  and sets our hearts aflame through the Spirit of Christ.
Mighty God,
  help us to catch a sense of your greatness,
  opening our hearts and minds to your presence
  made known through Father, Son and Holy Spirit.
Amen.

126

Mighty God,
  beyond all space and time,
  greater than our minds can grasp,
  ruler over all that is, has been and shall be –
  we worship you.
Loving Father,
  kind and merciful,
  full of goodness and compassion,
  constantly watching over us and directing our steps –
  we praise you.
Saviour Christ,
  flesh of our flesh yet the living image of God,
  sharing our humanity yet one with the Father,
  loving to the point of death yet bringer of life –
  we acknowledge you.
Holy Spirit,
  free and mysterious,
  source of guidance and inspiration,
  filling our hearts and mind –
  we welcome you.
Mighty God,
  Father, Son and Holy Spirit,
  with awe, joy and thanksgiving we celebrate all you mean to us
  and everything you have done in our lives.
To you be glory and honour,
  this and every day.
Amen.

127

Sovereign God,
> no one has ever beheld the fullness of your glory,
> for it is beyond human comprehension to take in.

Yet we thank you that, through Christ, you have made yourself known,
> revealing in him the full extent of your love;
> the wonder of your purpose,
> the awesomeness of your grace
> and the beauty of your truth.

Dwell in us now, through the Spirit of Christ,
> so that we may grow closer to him and closer to you.

Teach us to recognise your glory not just here but everywhere,
> not just today but every day,
> our hearts overwhelmed by your splendour
> and our souls giving you the glory,
> now and for evermore.

Amen.

All Saints' Day

128

Living God,
> we thank you for all those who have run the race
> and kept the faith before us;
> all whose example, across the centuries,
> has given encouragement and inspiration
> to your people in their personal journey of faith.

We thank you for those whose life and faith have spoken to us –
> uplifting, instructing, challenging and guiding,
> leading us forward into new experiences of your love.

Forgive us that we sometimes forget such examples,
> losing sight of all you have done and continue to do.

Help us to learn from the great company of saints to which we belong.

Speak,
> so that our love may grow,
> our faith be deepened
> and our resolve to serve you be strengthened.

So may we live always to your praise and glory,
> through Jesus Christ our Lord.

Amen.

Commitment

see also Discipleship, journey of; Palm Sunday

129

Gracious God,
    we have committed ourselves to your service,
    but we are all too aware of how weak that commitment is
    and how often we fail to honour it.
When our allegiance has been tested,
    our loyalty put on the line,
    we have repeatedly been found wanting,
    more concerned with our own interests than with serving Christ.
When discipleship has involved cost,
    and service meant putting ourselves out on behalf of others,
    our good intentions have swiftly evaporated,
    exposed as little more than fine-sounding ideas.
Gracious God,
    we want to serve you better,
    but we know that we will fail again,
    just as we have failed before,
    our faith flawed and our love imperfect.
Have mercy on us,
    and through Christ's faithfulness to the last
    inspire us to stay true to you
    whatever life may bring.
For his name's sake we pray.
Amen.

130

Lord Jesus Christ,
    we want to be true to our convictions,
    to stand up for what is right,
    but it's hard when the pressure is on.
It's hard not to bend when all around us disagree,
    not to compromise for the sake of peace,
    not to tone things down
    when we find ourselves in the firing line.
Yet there are times when we need to stick our necks out
    for what we believe in,
    even when doing so may make us unpopular with others.
Give us wisdom to know when those times are,
    and courage then to hold fast through them all.
Amen.

131
Sovereign God,
  you could have washed your hands of us,
  abandoned us to our fate,
  left us to struggle on in all our weakness, folly and failure.
But you didn't.
You spoke time and again through teachers, preachers, prophets,
  offering your word of life,
  and you spoke again, most powerfully, most wonderfully,
  through your Son, Jesus Christ.
You put words into action,
  love into practice,
  living and dying among us,
  bearing our sins,
  enduring our sorrow,
  dying our death so that we, in you, might live.
Sovereign God,
  you could so easily have put us second.
But you didn't –
  you put us first.
Teach us to put *you* first too.
Amen.

132
Living God,
  all too often we leave it to you to make the running in our relationship.
We are casual and complacent in discipleship,
  careless in making time to meet with you and forgetful of your love,
  yet we still expect you to be there when we need you,
  ready to answer our prayers and grant your blessing
  despite our slowness to serve you.
Forgive us for seeing faith as something given to us
  rather than as something we also need to work at.
Forgive us for seeing it as a one-off moment of conversion
  rather than a continuing story of commitment.
Teach us to make time to know you,
  to listen to your voice and to seek your will.
Deepen our experience of you in Christ,
  and so may we come to know you as a living reality in our lives
  and rejoice in all that you have done.
In the name of Christ, we ask it.
Amen.

133
Lord Jesus Christ,
   so often we let you down
   because we are not serious about following you.
Afraid of what unreserved commitment might involve,
   we tell ourselves that you will understand if we make compromises
   and tone down the message of the gospel;
   that you will make allowances for our mistakes,
   so we needn't try too hard to live up to your example.
Forgive us for abusing your grace and evading your challenge,
   for effectively denying your transforming power
   through the narrowness of our vision
   and the weakness of our faith.
Teach us to focus on your grace and goodness,
   so that, though we will never be quite like you,
   we may at least have the chance of getting closer.
In your name we ask it.
Amen.

134
Lord Jesus Christ,
   thank you for staying true to your calling to the very end,
   refusing to compromise your mission in any way.
Thank you for all those who have followed in your footsteps,
   giving their all for the sake of the gospel.
Teach us to walk faithfully in your way
   rather than follow the course of least resistance,
   to stand up for what we believe
   rather than go along with the crowd.
Help us to understand all you have done for us,
   and so may our lives be spent in your service,
   to the glory of your name.
Amen.

135
Lord Jesus Christ,
   we bear your name and we profess to follow your way,
   yet there is little if anything different about us from anyone else.
We have failed you in so many ways;
   our faith weak,
   our love poor
   and our commitment unpredictable.
We have been half-hearted in your service,
   concerned more about our own interests than your glory.
All too often our words say one thing but our deeds another,

the message we proclaim belied by the way we live,
    so that instead of leading people towards you we lead them away.
Forgive us and help us to follow you not just in name only but also in truth,
    proud to be identified with your cause
    and committing our lives to the work of your kingdom.
We ask it for your name's sake.
Amen.

136

Lord Jesus Christ,
    we talk about belonging to you and offering you our service,
    but so often reality falls short of the ideal.
Instead of making you an integral part of our lives,
    we treat you as an optional extra,
    there to turn to as and when it suits us.
Instead of working for your kingdom,
    we strive solely to serve our own interests.
Instead of involving ourselves in the life of your people,
    we stay on the fringes,
    reluctant to commit ourselves wholly to your cause.
Our deeds deny our words;
    our lives betray our lack of faith.
Forgive us and save us from confusing nominal Christianity
    with living discipleship.
Teach us what it means to belong to you
    and to be part of your Church,
    and so may we serve you as you deserve,
    to the glory of your name.
Amen.

137

Lord Jesus Christ,
    we want to commit ourselves to your service
    and we do our best to follow you,
    but we are led astray so easily,
    our faith so weak and temptation so strong.
We think we have turned our back on our old ways,
    only to find them resurfacing in another guise.
We try to let go of self,
    only to discover it still holds us firmly in its grip.
For all our good intentions,
    we find ourselves caught between two worlds,
    unable to escape the hold of one
    yet incapable of fully embracing the other.

Forgive us the many times we fail you,
   and give us strength,
   when our allegiance is tested,
   to put you first.
Help us not simply to call you Lord,
   but to make you the Lord of our lives,
   to the glory of your name.
Amen.

138
Lord Jesus Christ,
   when we think of your commitment to us
   and your willingness to face suffering and death on our behalf,
   we are ashamed of our disloyalty to you
   and our failure to stand up for your kingdom.
We keep quiet about our faith for fear of embarrassment.
We close our eyes and ears to wrongdoing,
   rather than risk unpopularity.
We water down our principles for the sake of an easy peace.
We avoid getting involved in needs around us,
   claiming they are none of our business.
In so many ways, we let you down,
   offering you an empty, secret discipleship.
Forgive us our weakness and cowardice,
   and give us courage to stand up for what we believe in
   and proudly to declare you as Lord of our lives,
   to the glory of your name.
Amen.

139
Lord Jesus Christ,
   you tell us to walk in the light,
   and to witness to it through the things we do
   and the people we are.
You call us to let your light shine through us
   so that others might see and give glory to God.
Forgive us that all too often we do the opposite,
   hiding our light under a bushel,
   even sometimes to the point of secret discipleship.
Afraid of what others might think
   and concerned that admitting faith in you
   might prejudice our standing in this world,
   we keep our beliefs private.
Forgive us the feebleness of our commitment
   and the weakness of our love.

Help us to recognise everything you have done for us,
   and so teach us to acknowledge you proudly
   as the light of our lives,
   whatever the cost might be.
In your name we pray.
Amen.

140
Loving God,
   you ask us whatever we do,
   to do it for your sake –
   to offer our whole life,
   our every thought,
   word and action –
   to your service and for your glory.
Help us to understand what that really means –
   to see every part of each day as an opportunity to work for you.
Teach us to do everything in such a way
   that your hand may be evident upon us,
   your Spirit unmistakably at work
   and your love clear to all,
   to the glory of your name.
Amen.

141
Sovereign God,
   we say we love you
   yet all too often our lives say something else.
We are casual and careless in our relationship with you,
   relegating you to the periphery of our lives
   instead of placing you at the centre.
We make time for you as an afterthought,
   fitting you in as and when the opportunity arises,
   and if we cannot find time,
   we lose little sleep over the matter.
Our prayer life is erratic,
   our study of your word lackadaisical,
   our commitment half-hearted.
Forgive us for imagining this is sufficient,
   for somehow thinking that our relationship with you can take care of itself.
Forgive us for loving you so little
   and then wondering why we do not feel as close to you as we should.
Teach us what it means to love you with body, mind and soul,
   and help us to be as committed to you as you are to us,
   through Jesus Christ our Lord.
Amen.

Confession and forgiveness

Acknowledging our faults

142

Lord Jesus Christ,
    we do not mean to be self-righteous but we *can* be,
    more often than we realise.
We speak of humility,
    of being wholly dependent on your grace,
    yet we presume to pass judgement on others.
We claim to recognise our faults,
    but if anyone points them out to us we are quick to take offence.
We see the speck in our neighbour's eye
    but repeatedly overlook the log in our own.
Forgive any tendency to assume that we are right and others are wrong.
Help us, instead, to understand that we depend finally on your grace,
    and so, recognising the strengths and weaknesses of all,
    may we live in true humility,
    to the glory of your name.
Amen.

143

Lord,
    we don't like being wrong.
It hurts our pride
    and goes against the grain to admit we've made a mistake.
We prefer to blame somebody else,
    to look for an excuse that justifies our actions,
    but though we may fool ourselves,
    we can never fool you.
Forgive us, Lord, for those times we have shifted the blame on to others.
Forgive us for hiding behind falsehoods and half-truths,
    letting excuses become so much part of us
    that we no longer realise we are making them.
Teach us to act wisely and with integrity;
    and when we go wrong,
    give us courage to admit it
    and humility to accept our dependence on your unfailing grace.
Amen.

144

Loving God,
    we usually know when we have done wrong
    but we very rarely admit it.

We are reluctant to lose face,
　　so we go on pretending,
　　adding one falsehood to another.
Yet there can be no peace that way,
　　no prospect of inner contentment.
Give us the wisdom and the humility we need
　　to recognise our mistakes,
　　to acknowledge them openly,
　　to seek forgiveness,
　　and, where possible, to make amends,
　　through Jesus Christ our Lord.
Amen.

145
Loving God,
　　we know what we should be and we know what we are,
　　the gulf between the two so wide.
So we come now in shame and sorrow before you,
　　seeking your mercy.
Forgive us everything that disfigures our life:
　　the pride, greed, selfishness and envy
　　that alienate us not only from ourselves and others
　　but also, and above all,
　　from you.
Forgive us our unkind words,
　　foolish deeds
　　and unworthy thoughts;
　　our weakness of will
　　and carelessness in discipleship.
Work within us
　　and, by your grace,
　　make us whole,
　　through Jesus Christ our Lord.
Amen.

146
Gracious God,
　　we are not bad at confessing our mistakes to you,
　　but we are hopeless when it comes to confessing them to others.
We make excuses for our behaviour rather than admit the truth;
　　we prevaricate and deceive,
　　rather than acknowledge our weakness.
Instead of admitting where we've gone wrong and seeking forgiveness,
　　we go on digging an ever-deeper hole for ourselves,
　　making it harder and harder to go back and start again.

Give us courage when we fail
   to confess our mistakes to those affected by our actions,
   and help us to do all in our power to make amends.
Teach us to face the truth so that it may set us free,
   in Christ's name.
Amen.

147
Lord,
   it isn't easy to face the truth
   for there is much we prefer to hide
   from ourselves as well as others.
We are ashamed of our many failings –
   the way we so easily succumb to temptation
   and so often fail to honour you.
We talk of strength,
   but show weakness.
We speak of serving others,
   but have time only for ourselves.
We preach forgiveness,
   but are swift in practice to judge.
Though we have caught a glimpse of what life could be
   the reality is that we fall pathetically short,
   yet we keep up a façade for the world rather than admit the facts.
Lord,
   you see us as we are,
   for there can be nothing hidden from you,
   and yet still you love us.
Give us courage, then, to face ourselves honestly,
   and to acknowledge our faults,
   so that we may know the forgiveness you offer
   and rejoice in renewal of life,
   through Jesus Christ our Lord.
Amen.

148
Gracious God,
   you know how much we want to serve you.
We have resolved to live more faithfully so many times
   that we have lost count,
   yet, somehow, when the moment of challenge comes,
   we are found wanting.
Despite the good we long to do,
   we fall victim yet again to the same old weaknesses,
   unable to conquer the feebleness of our sinful nature.

Have mercy, O God,
  and renew us through your Holy Spirit.
Cleanse us through the love of Christ,
  and put a new heart and a right spirit within us,
    through Jesus Christ our Lord.
Amen.

149
Living God,
  there is so much in our lives that is not as it should be,
  yet all too often we stubbornly refuse to admit it.
We pretend that nothing much is wrong;
  that any minor aberrations are superficial,
  hardly worth bothering about.
Even when we are more honest with ourselves,
  we still believe that we can put matters right through our own efforts;
  that all it needs is a greater resolve on our part.
Yet, despite all our attempts to start afresh,
  the old mistakes and weaknesses soon show through,
  as unsightly as ever.
Teach us that we need your help if we seriously hope ever to change.
Take us and mould us in your hands,
  re-creating us from within,
  so that, by the grace of Christ,
  we may be the person you would have us be.
Amen.

150
Sovereign God,
  we find it so hard to acknowledge our mistakes,
  to admit that we are as fallible as the next person.
We know we have done wrong,
  our errors all too evident,
  yet we run from the truth,
  unwilling or afraid to face facts.
We deny our faults or attempt to excuse them.
We concern ourselves with outer appearances rather than with inner reality,
  attempting to convince ourselves that all is well,
  even though we know in our hearts that all is not as it should be.
Forgive us our dishonesty and cowardice.
Help us not just to take the easy way out in confessing our mistakes to you
  but also to confess them to others
  so that we may be able to put them behind us and start afresh,
    through Jesus Christ our Lord.
Amen.

Forgiveness of God

151

Gracious God,
    once more we thank you for the wonder of your love
    and the awesome extent of your mercy.
We have failed you in so much,
    repeatedly ignoring your will and breaking your commandments,
    yet, despite our betrayal,
    you not only forgive but also put our mistakes behind us.
However often we go astray,
    however great our faults
    and however feeble the love we show in return,
    you are always willing to forget and move on.
Teach us the secret of such love.
Touch our hearts with your goodness
    and so may we learn to let go of past hurts
    and build instead for the future.
May we be agents of your healing, redeeming and renewing grace,
    to the glory of your name.
Amen.

152

Gracious God,
    though we try to put the past behind us,
    all too often we are haunted by mistakes.
Though we try to make amends for the wrongs we've done,
    we find it hard to escape a sense of guilt.
Remind us that you are always ready to offer free and total forgiveness,
    no matter how foolish we have been
    or how many opportunities we have wasted.
Teach us that the past is done with
    and the future is open before us.
Receive, then, our thanks and lead us forward,
    in the name of Christ.
Amen.

153

Living God,
    though we have let you down in so many ways,
    teach us that you do not judge as we do,
    but that you are truly willing to forgive and forget.
Teach us to put the past behind us
    and to accept the new life you so freely offer,
    and so may we live each day as your gift,
    nurtured by the love of Christ

and renewed through your Holy Spirit,
   to your praise and glory.
Amen.

154
Lord Jesus Christ,
   you have called us to faith
   and gratefully we have responded,
   committing ourselves to walking your way,
   yet we are conscious of our repeated failure,
   our inability to keep faith.
We mean to follow,
   but we are weak and foolish,
   so easily deflected from our path,
   and eventually we despair of ever staying on our chosen course.
Assure us at such times that your patience is never exhausted,
   your love never withdrawn
   and your grace never denied.
Teach us that you long to lead us forward again,
   waiting only for us to acknowledge where we have gone wrong
   and to reach out in faith for your forgiveness.
So we come,
   in true repentance,
   asking you to turn us round
   and lead us forward,
   in your strength
   and for your name's sake.
Amen.

155
Loving God,
   there are some things in our past we would rather forget
   but that return to haunt us –
   foolish actions,
   hasty words,
   evil thoughts,
   wasted opportunities –
   things we should have done but haven't
   or that we shouldn't have done but have.
We find it hard to forgive ourselves,
   harder still to think that others can do so,
   and hardest of all to believe that you can ever forgive us.
Yet, though we may condemn ourselves,
   and others may do the same,
   you repeatedly show us how you are able to change lives,
   not just forgiving past mistakes

but also making people new,
   renewing them from within through your Holy Spirit.
Help us, then, to bring all the feelings of guilt and shame
   that hold us down,
   and to open our lives to your renewing touch in Christ,
   for in his name we ask it.
Amen.

156

Merciful God,
   unlike us you don't dwell on past failures.
Instead, you invite us to acknowledge them openly before you,
   to receive your pardon and then to move on.
Teach us to do just that –
   to accept your offer for what it is
   and, rather than wallow in our guilt,
   to rejoice in your mercy.
Teach us to let go of the recriminations, doubt and fears that hold us captive
   and to accept the freedom you have won for us.
Help us not simply to talk about new life
   but to live it joyfully,
   receiving each moment as your gracious gift,
   through Jesus Christ our Lord.
Amen.

157

Sovereign God,
   we thank you that you judge not by the outside
   but by the person underneath;
   not simply by our faithless actions
   but by our underlying desire to serve you.
Where we are swift to condemn,
   you are looking to forgive.
You are always ready to show mercy,
   to believe in our potential
   rather than dwell on our past record.
Save us from interpreting your judgement
   in terms of our own narrow horizons;
   from attributing to you a strictness
   that reflects our own narrow outlook
   and that denies your grace.
Teach us to receive your forgiveness
   and to rejoice in the newness of life you long to bring,
   through Jesus Christ our Lord.
Amen.

Forgiving others

158
Gracious God,
   we don't find it easy to give someone a second chance,
   especially when they've let us down personally.
It's hard to overcome feelings of hurt and anger,
   and harder still ever to trust that person in the way we used to.
Yet you go on giving us another chance day after day,
   and, despite our repeated failure,
   you are willing still to trust us with the work of your kingdom.
Teach us, then, instead of dwelling on faults,
   to look for strengths;
   instead of putting people down,
   to lift them up;
   and instead of consigning them to the scrap heap,
   to give them the benefit of the doubt.
Help us to forgive others as you forgive us,
   in Christ's name.
Amen.

159
Gracious God,
   we have no reason to expect your mercy,
   for though we say we are sorry
   we go on letting you down time after time,
   making the same mistakes we have always made,
   ignoring your will,
   even wilfully rejecting your guidance.
Yet you go on forgiving us,
   year in, year out,
   always ready to receive us back and to help us start again.
We praise you for the wonder of your love,
   your goodness that is never exhausted.
Help us, having been forgiven so much,
   to forgive others, whose mistakes are so little by comparison.
Give us generous hearts and graciousness of spirit,
   so that we do not simply speak of forgiveness
   but also display the truth of it in our lives,
   through Jesus Christ our Lord.
Amen.

160
Gracious God,
   you tell us that as we forgive so we shall be forgiven,
   and the thought of that is frightening,

for we find forgiving others so very difficult.
When we are hurt,
    insulted,
    let down,
    our natural inclination is to want revenge,
    and we allow that thirst to fester within us
    until it grows out of all proportion to the wrong we have suffered.
Teach us to leave vengeance to you,
    knowing that in your own time justice will be done.
Amen.

161

Almighty God,
    we have no claim on your love
    and no right to expect forgiveness,
    yet you constantly reach out in love,
    eager to forgive and forget.
Day after day,
    your nature is to have mercy,
    putting the past behind us
    and helping us to begin again.
We thank you for the awesomeness of your love
    and we ask for your help in opening our lives to your redeeming grace.
Teach us to confess our sins
    and to commit ourselves again to your service,
    and so may we receive the cleansing, renewal and forgiveness
    you alone can bring.
We ask it in the name of Christ,
    our Lord and Saviour.
Amen.

162

Gracious God,
    we have so much to thank you for,
    and yet there are times when we lose sight of that,
    dwelling instead on the disappointments and frustrations of life.
We brood about the things that didn't work out as we hoped,
    the hurts inflicted upon us,
    the mistakes made,
    the opportunities denied,
    and we allow these to fester within us,
    poisoning us from within,
    eating away at our happiness until we think of nothing else.
Forgive us our foolishness
    and help us to regain a proper sense of proportion.

Teach us to put the past behind us
and to embrace the present moment,
recognising that what's done is done
but that you are constantly making all things new.
Save us from that sourness of spirit that accomplishes nothing
and that finally will serve only to destroy us.
In Christ's name we pray.
Amen.

Grace

163
Living God,
we thank you for your amazing grace,
your love of us as we are,
despite all our faults and weaknesses.
We praise you that you accept us
not through our own efforts
or according to our own deserving,
but through faith in Christ.
Forgive us for abusing that truth sometimes,
throwing your love back into your face through taking it for granted.
Forgive us for assuming sometimes we can carry on regardless,
secure in the knowledge of your mercy.
Give us a longing to serve you better
and to grow in the likeness of Christ,
not in any attempt to justify ourselves
but simply to express our love for you.
Fill us now with your Spirit,
and so help us to live each day in newness of life,
to the glory of your name.
Amen.

164
Gracious God,
there are many ready to sneer at faith,
imagining that we consider ourselves special,
in some way holier or better than others,
but we know the reality is so very different:
your love for us not something we deserve
but solely down to your grace.
We recognise our faults,
we acknowledge our sinfulness,
and we realise full well that we will never be anywhere near perfect.
Save us, then, from ever appearing self-righteousness
or judgemental towards others.

Teach us, rather, to live as those who recognise
    your love and acceptance of all,
    and may such openness characterise our attitude in all our dealings,
    to the glory of your name.
Amen.

165
Almighty God,
    we have no claim on your love,
    no reason to feel we deserve it,
    for we are false and faithless in so much,
    but we want to know and serve you better,
    to glimpse your glory,
    understand your greatness
    and receive your blessing.
We want to taste more of your goodness
    experience more of your grace,
    and experience your healing, renewing power within us,
    and so we come,
    resolved to take hold of the new life you have promised.
Respond to us, we pray,
    and, as we have come to you,
    so come to us,
    through Jesus Christ our Lord.
Amen.

166
Gracious God,
    we have no claim on your goodness,
    no reason to expect your mercy.
Despite our best intentions,
    we repeatedly fail you,
    preferring our way to yours.
We say one thing,
    yet do another;
    we claim to love you,
    yet openly flout your will.
Forgive us,
    for, try as we might, we cannot help ourselves.
Renew us through your Spirit,
    redeem us through the grace of Christ,
    and remake us through your great love,
    so that we might live and work for you,
    to the glory of your name.
Amen.

167

Living God,
   we know that we have no claim on your love
   and no reason to expect your goodness,
   for we fail you day after day,
   week after week,
   yet we celebrate once more the glorious truth
   that you love and accept us as we are.
Though we deserve so little,
   you give us so much;
   though we serve you so poorly,
   you bless us so richly,
   your grace never exhausted,
   your love refusing to be denied.
We know that we can never earn such love
   or ever begin to repay it,
   but we praise you that you do not ask us to,
   your gift of new life in Christ truly being free.
Help us, then,
   humbly, gladly and gratefully,
   to receive what you offer,
   and to give you the glory.
Amen.

168

Living God,
   we praise you for calling us into the fellowship of your people.
We rejoice in everything that means:
   that you did not just accept us because you had to,
   because no one else would respond;
   that you did not accept us reluctantly,
   hesitant because of our faults and weaknesses;
   and that you did not accept us provisionally,
   dependent upon whether we measure up to your expectations.
Instead, we know that you welcome us
   freely, gladly and unequivocally,
   opening your heart to us without reserve,
   glad to embrace us as your children
   and proud to call us your family.
For the wonder of that truth,
   we offer our grateful worship,
   in the name of Christ.
Amen.

169
Living God,
    when we look at our lives,
    we see so much that is wrong
    and so little that is right.
We see selfishness and greed,
    envy and bitterness,
    rather than the fruits of the Spirit that we so much long to show.
We see narrowness of mind,
    weakness of faith and feebleness of commitment
    rather than the vision, trust and dedication that you expect from us.
We want to live and work for you,
    yet we seem incapable of doing so,
    and we despair of ever changing.
Help us to remember that you can achieve
    what we cannot hope to do by ourselves;
    that you love us and died for us even before we knew you.
Teach us that *you* believe in us,
    even when *we* don't.
In Christ's name we pray.
Amen.

170
Loving God,
    we do not know why we go astray,
    for we want so much to stay true.
We yearn to offer you faithful and committed service,
    but somehow we always fall short,
    and we fear sometimes that one day even *your* love will be exhausted,
    our disobedience pushing your patience too far.
Remind us, at such times,
    of your infinite grace that goes on reaching out to us,
    come what may.
Remind us that you are a God always ready to forgive and forget,
    longing to lift us up and carry us safely home on your shoulders.
In Christ's name we thank you.
Amen.

171
Lord Jesus Christ,
    you chose Peter to be the rock of your Church –
    the man who, for all his protestations of loyalty,
    misunderstood and denied you.
Across the centuries you have similarly chosen
    ordinary, weak human beings to be your followers,
    well aware that most will fail you when put to the test.

We thank you that you call us in turn,
  knowing that we are weak, foolish and fallible
  yet loving us just the same.
Lord,
  we praise you that though we see so little good within ourselves,
  you see those worth dying for
  and worth sharing life with for all eternity.
Amen.

172
Almighty God,
  you are greater than our minds can imagine,
  sovereign over history,
  the Creator of the ends of the earth,
  and yet you have time for each one of us.
You are all good,
  all true,
  all holy,
  all righteous,
  and yet you accept us with our many imperfections.
You are the source of love,
  the fount of knowledge,
  the giver of life,
  the one who gives meaning to the universe,
  and yet you delight in our companionship.
Almighty God,
  such things are too wonderful for us,
  too awesome to take in.
  We marvel at your grace,
  we rejoice in your goodness
  and we offer now our worship,
  through Jesus Christ our Lord.
Amen.

173
Gracious God,
  we thank you for the awesomeness of your love
  and the wonder of your grace.
Day after day,
  you show us mercy,
  accepting our feeble faith and hesitant discipleship,
  understanding our weakness,
  putting our faults behind us
  and helping us to start again.
However much we fail you,
  your patience is never exhausted,

your love refuses to be denied.
We deserve so little,
   yet you give so much;
   our love is so weak,
   yet you respond so richly;
   our faith is so small,
   yet you bless us so constantly.
Gracious God,
   if you dealt with us according to our deserving
   we could not hope to escape punishment,
   for we have failed you in ways too many to number,
   but your grace is greater than we can begin to imagine.
For your love that embraces all,
   and continues for eternity,
   we praise you,
   in the name of Christ.
Amen.

174

Gracious God,
   despite our repeated disobedience,
   your love continues undiminished,
   reaching out to us every moment of every day.
Despite rejection by the world,
   still you go on seeking to draw us to yourself,
   until every broken relationship with you is mended.
So it is now and so it has always been from the beginning of time,
   your nature always to have mercy.
Help us to appreciate the enormity of your faithfulness,
   and to open our hearts more fully to your grace,
   through Jesus Christ our Lord.
Amen.

175

Living God,
   you know us inside out down to the last detail.
You see us not as we would like to be,
   nor as we pretend to be,
   but as we are:
   the good and the bad,
   the faithful and the unfaithful,
   the lovely and the unlovely.
We can never deceive you as to the truth,
   never hide the reality of who we are behind a public face,
   yet, despite all our faults,
   still you love us.

Living God,
    remembering that truth,
    help us to be honest with you,
    confessing our faults,
    acknowledging our weaknesses
    and seeking your grace,
    through Jesus Christ our Lord.
Amen.

176
Lord Jesus Christ,
    you paid the price that we could never begin to pay.
You gave your all to cancel the debt we owe,
    securing our freedom through your suffering and death.
We celebrate again the awesomeness of that sacrifice
    and the generosity of that gift,
    and we praise you that you make no extortionate demands
    in return for forgiveness,
    nor impose stringent conditions before you are ready to grant it.
You ask us simply to acknowledge our need
    and to accept your mercy,
    trusting in what you have done on our behalf.
Lord Jesus Christ,
    such grace is beyond our comprehension,
    but we respond to it with joyful praise and heartfelt worship,
    offering you our love and service,
    not as a repayment but as a token of our glad thanksgiving.
To you be glory and honour,
    blessing and adoration,
    now and for evermore.
Amen.

177
Lord,
    we need your love,
    your mercy,
    your guidance
    and your peace,
    for without you our souls are restless,
    our lives impoverished
    and our destiny hopeless.
But we thank you too
    that, incredibly, you are a God who has need of us,
    a God who has chosen to make yourself
    dependent on human cooperation.

You need our faith and trust;
  our hands and feet;
  our willingness to speak in service and witness;
  our commitment to you in body, mind and soul.
Living God,
  we marvel that you need us as much as we need you,
  but we thank you for that great truth,
  that awesome privilege
  and that amazing responsibility.
Help us to honour the trust you have placed in us,
  through honouring Jesus Christ our Lord.
In his name we pray.
Amen.

178
Loving God,
  time and again we have gone astray from you;
  time and again you have come looking for us,
  putting us on your shoulders and carrying us home.
We tell ourselves that next time it will be different,
  next time we'll stay true,
  but that's not what happens:
  still we wander from your side.
We are weak and foolish,
  undeserving of your love,
  yet still you reach out in love,
  drawing us back to you.
We praise you for the wonder of your grace,
  for your willingness to lay down your Son for the life of the world.
We thank you for your constant provision of all our needs.
Have mercy on our repeated failures,
  and continue to guide us,
  watching over us even when we lose sight of you.
In the name of Jesus,
  the shepherd of all,
  lead us on through the changes and chances of this life,
  and through the valley of the shadow of death,
  until we are safely gathered into your kingdom
  and the journey is done.
Amen.

179
Sovereign God,
  if you treated us as we deserve,
  none could stand before you,
  but you are a God of infinite mercy,

full of love and goodness.
You came to our world in Christ,
    and you died for us while we were yet sinners.
You reached out through him
    to those who knew themselves to be unworthy,
    deserving of punishment,
    yet, through your grace,
    you brought acceptance, wholeness and renewal.
So now we open our lives to your generous pardon,
    your unfailing love
    and your undeserved blessing.
Receive our praise
    for all you so freely and wonderfully give in Christ,
    for his name's sake.
Amen.

Cost of discipleship

see also Commitment

180

Gracious God,
  we forget sometimes that alongside the blessings of discipleship
  there is always the cost –
  sacrifices that will be asked of us;
  demands upon our time, energy, gifts and money;
  responsibilities we will be asked to accept.
Help us to respond gladly to whatever you may ask,
  knowing that, however great the price may be,
  the rewards are infinitely worth it.
Teach us to offer to you all that you ask from us,
  until that day when we rejoice in everything you hold in store
  for all your people.
All this we ask through Jesus Christ our Lord.
Amen.

181

Living God,
  it is uncomfortable sometimes having to choose.
We prefer to sit on the fence,
  to hedge our bets,
  to take the path of compromise in the hope of pleasing all.
Even when we know the right way,
  we turn aside from it,
  fearful of the cost that may be involved.
Yet, deep down, we know this simply won't do;
  that failing to decide for you means deciding against you.
Help us to recognise when we need to make a choice,
  and then give us courage to stand firm in faith,
  whatever it may cost.
Amen.

182

Lord Jesus Christ,
  it is easy to talk of taking up our cross and following you,
  but the reality is different.
We find it hard to deny ourselves even a little,
  let alone to give our all.
There is so much we want to enjoy,
  so much we want to achieve,

and the thought of sacrificing any of that
   is one we would rather push aside.
Yet you have taught that it is in losing our lives we truly find them,
   and that we shall find lasting treasures not on earth but in heaven.
Help us, then, instead of clinging slavishly to self-interest,
   to give of ourselves freely,
   just as you gave yourself for us.
Amen.

183
Lord Jesus Christ,
   faced with difficult decisions
   so often we tell ourselves we have no choice,
   that life has pushed us into a corner,
   leaving us no alternative as to how to act.
But in our hearts we know that isn't so.
It may be hard, painful or costly,
   but finally there is always a right way
   if we are prepared to look for it.
Forgive us for all the excuses we make.
Forgive us for the ways we wriggle and squirm
   rather than face up to our responsibilities.
Forgive us for all the times we have taken the soft option
   rather than the one we know to be right.
Teach us, next time we have to make a choice,
   to seek your will,
   to listen to your voice
   and to respond in faith,
   to the glory of your name.
Amen.

Sacrifice and self-denial
see also Christian seasons: Lent; Serving others

184
Lord Jesus,
   throughout your life you were the man for others,
   always ready to listen,
   always prepared to respond,
   whatever the cost to yourself.
At your death it was the same –
   still you poured yourself out,
   thinking of others to the last.
Forgive us that we are the opposite,
   more often than not our thoughts only for self,
   rarely willing to listen,

even less so to respond,
   fearful of what it all might cost us.
Throughout our lives we are the same,
   reluctant to give of ourselves,
   thinking of our own interests to the last.
We do not mean to do it,
   but it is the way we are,
   hard though we try to be different.
Lord Jesus,
   forgive us and teach us your way,
   for until we learn to be the servant of all
   we will continue to be the slave of self.
Help us to give freely,
   and in a life of service to find true freedom.
Amen.

185

Lord Jesus Christ,
   we praise you for your ministry,
   your love,
   your faithfulness to your calling.
We thank you for your willingness to face even death itself
   so that we might find the true meaning of life.
We thank you for that sense of purpose,
   that inner courage,
   that deep faith which gave you the strength
   to continue on your chosen path
   to the very end.
Lord Jesus Christ,
   forgive us that having received so much we give so little in return.
Forgive us that we shy away from sacrifice and self-denial.
Forgive us for taking the easy and less costly way
   rather than the way of the cross.
Help us to deny ourselves
   and so to find life in all its fullness.
In your name we ask it.
Amen.

186

Gracious God,
   forgive us our mean and selfish spirit –
   our desire so often to safeguard pleasures for ourselves,
   to provide for our own well-being while ignoring the needs of others.
Teach us that it is in giving we receive,
   in denying ourselves that we discover true riches.

Help us not just to assent to that truth intellectually,
  but also to believe it in our hearts and show it in our lives.
Give us a heart overflowing with generosity,
  eager to share with others the good things you have given us,
  and so may we add both to their joy and to our own,
  through Jesus Christ our Lord.
Amen.

187
Lord Jesus Christ,
  no one can ever give us more than you have given,
  for you have blessed us with life itself –
  life overflowing with good things,
  life eternal –
  and to make that gift possible you gave of yourself,
  not just a little but all.
You bore the limitations of human flesh;
  you endured rejection,
  humiliation
  and, finally, death on a cross;
  and,
  most awesome of all,
  you took on yourself the dreadful burden of this world's sinfulness,
  experiencing despair and isolation for our sakes.
Forgive us that, despite all this,
  we give so grudgingly in return.
Forgive us that though our words say one thing
  our lives say another;
  that our thoughts are so little for you
  and still less for others.
Help us to catch again a glimpse of the love you have so freely given
  and so may we spontaneously give of ourselves
  in joyful and heartfelt thanksgiving,
  for your name's sake.
Amen.

188
Living God,
  you challenge us to go the extra mile,
  to do more than anyone can ask or expect of us.
Forgive us that we find that so hard:
  that we prefer to do as little as possible rather than as much;
  that we give our help, time, service and money
  grudgingly rather than cheerfully.
We praise you for the readiness of Christ to go not just the extra mile
  but to give his all,

identifying himself with our human condition,
willingly experiencing suffering and death
so that we might discover life in its fullness.
We praise you for those who have followed in his footsteps,
willing to go beyond the call of duty in the service of others.
Touch our hearts through their example
and inspire us through the love of Christ,
so that we may be more ready to do that little bit extra,
to go beyond people's expectations,
to give as you have given to us so freely.
In the name of Christ we ask it.
Amen.

189
Lord Jesus Christ,
we want to follow your example
and we strive to do so,
but so often our weakness gets the better of us.
We talk of serving others
but live instead for ourselves;
we speak of self-sacrifice
but indulge our self-interest;
we profess loyalty to your cause,
yet repeatedly deny it through the way we live.
We have preferred our ways to yours,
more concerned with our own advancement than your kingdom.
We have been weak in our commitment
and half-hearted in offering our service.
Forgive us all the ways our lives fail to reflect your goodness
and all the ways our faithlessness betrays your grace.
Touch our lives afresh
and fill our hearts with your love
so that we may truly live for you,
making known your love
and bringing closer your kingdom.
In your name we ask it.
Amen.

190
Lord Jesus Christ,
we want to serve you,
and we like to believe we do,
but unwittingly we can turn even our faith into a way of serving ourselves.
We gain strength through fellowship and worship,
but neglect your call to mission.

We focus on our own concerns in prayer
  and forget about the world beyond.
Even our deeds of kindness
  can finally be more about our own sense of righteousness
  than the needs of those we think we are serving.
Lord Jesus,
  overcome the stranglehold of self
  and help us to understand that true discipleship brings its own reward,
  for the more we give the more we shall receive.
In your mercy,
  hear our prayer.
Amen.

191
Lord Jesus Christ,
  we are good at talking about service
  but not very good at showing it.
We speak of your love for the helpless and hopeless,
  but we all too rarely translate concern into action.
Forgive us the way we have neglected opportunities
  to help others,
  through deeds large or small.
Forgive the selfishness that has obscured love,
  the greed that has denied compassion
  and the laziness of body, mind and spirit
  that has so often prevented any meaningful response.
Show us where and how we can serve in your name,
  and inspire us to reach out in love,
  offering something of ourselves to others,
  even as you offered your all for us.
By your grace we ask it.
Amen.

_____Creation, stewardship of _____

192
Lord of all,
  we forget sometimes that your love involves responsibility
  as well as privilege;
  a duty not just to you but to the whole of your creation,
  to nurture and protect rather than simply exploit it.
Forgive us our part in a society that has too often lived for today
  with no thought of tomorrow.
Forgive us our unquestioning acceptance of an economic system
  that plunders this world's resources
  with little regard as to the consequences.
Help us to live less wastefully
  and with more thought for those who will come after us.
Challenge the hearts and minds of people everywhere,
  that both they and we may understand more fully
  the wonder and the fragility of this planet you have given us,
  and so honour our calling to be faithful stewards of it all,
  in Christ's name.
Amen.

193
Lord of all,
  we praise you for the universe in all its wonder,
  for the world in all its beauty
  and for life itself in all its incredible variety.
There is so much that gives us pleasure,
  offers fulfilment
  and captures our imagination;
  so much that challenges and inspires,
  speaking now of your wonderful love
  and causing us to look forward with anticipation.
Forgive us for so often abusing all you have given –
  despoiling this world,
  failing to appreciate it as we should,
  treating it as ours by right rather than entrusted as your gift.
Open our eyes to the countless blessings
  and inexhaustible riches you have so freely given,
  and help us to show our appreciation
  by safeguarding them for future
  generations to enjoy in turn,
  in Christ's name.
Amen.

194
Loving God,
   we thank you for the wonder of the universe
   and the infinite beauty of this world.
We praise you for the loveliness that surrounds us,
   the inexhaustible splendour of creation.
Forgive us for becoming over-familiar with it all,
   exploiting and squandering your many gifts.
Help us to rejoice in all you have given
      and to act as faithful stewards of creation,
      to the glory of your name.
Amen.

_____ Daily life, finding God in _____

195
Creator God,
  we thank you for the world you have given us:
  so full of beauty,
  so touched with wonder.
We praise you for its ability to move, astound and refresh us,
  and above all for the way it speaks of your love and purpose.
Forgive us that we sometimes lose sight of those deeper realities,
  failing to look beneath the surface.
Open our eyes afresh,
  and help us to see your hand in creation
  and your love in the daily routine of life,
  through Jesus Christ our Lord.
Amen.

196
Living God,
  we thank you that before ever we thought of seeking you,
  you sought us;
  that you had time for us
  even when we lived only for ourselves.
Teach us that you are constantly at work in our lives,
  even though we may not always see it,
  speaking through people we meet
  and moving in each and every situation
  to challenge,
  guide,
  confront
  or inspire.
Open our eyes to see you
  and our hearts to respond,
  so that we may live and work for your glory.,
  through Jesus Christ our Lord.
Amen.

197
Living God,
  we thank you for opportunities to share in the worship of your people
  and to focus our thoughts on your presence,
  but save us from mistakenly imagining
  you are more present in worship than anywhere else.
Teach us that you are by our side
  wherever we may be

and whatever we may be doing,
    involved in every aspect of our lives
    and in every part of the world.
May that knowledge illumine the affairs of each day
    and enrich each moment
    as we realise that you are constantly waiting to meet with us,
    speak to us,
    lead us
    and bless us.
Teach us to consecrate not just a few moments each week
    but all of our lives,
    to your service
    and to your glory.
In Christ's name.
Amen.

198

Living God,
    you are at work in so many ways,
    if we could only see it.
Forgive us everything that blinds us to the breadth of your activity –
    our closed mind and rigid preconceptions,
    our limited understanding and lack of faith,
    our asking the wrong questions,
    and our looking in the wrong places for the wrong things.
Open our eyes to your presence,
    our minds to your truth,
    and our souls to your Spirit,
    and so may we glimpse you in the daily events of life
    and in the affairs of the world,
    this and every day,
    in Christ's name.
Amen.

199

Loving God,
    we thank you for the gift of sight;
    for everything of beauty, inspiration and interest that we see each day.
Forgive us, though, that too often we see only with our eyes,
    failing to look beneath the surface to deeper truths underneath.
Open then our souls,
    so that we may see where you would lead us
    and look at the world in a new light,
    through Jesus Christ our Lord.
Amen.

_____ Discipleship, journey of _____

see also Adversity, faith in; Commitment

200

Lord Jesus Christ,
   you call us to walk in faith,
   but we so rarely do that.
We follow for a time,
   but we are quickly led astray.
When your message is too demanding,
   when you ask from us what we would rather not give,
   and when your words make us feel uncomfortable,
   striking too near the mark,
   then we turn away from you,
   resisting your call.
When other interests conflict with discipleship,
   when the demands and responsibilities of each day crowd in upon us,
   we are swift to forget you,
   ignoring your will in preference to our own.
When life is hard and things do not go as we had hoped,
   faith gives way to doubt and we lose sight of your promises.
Forgive that shallowness of our commitment,
   and grant light to our path,
   so that we may step forward in faith
   and travel onwards wherever you might lead,
   through Jesus Christ our Lord.
Amen.

201

Gracious God,
   we thank you for the great adventure of life
   in all its endless diversity and richness.
We thank you that there is always more to learn,
   more to explore
   and more to experience.
Keep our minds open to that special truth
   for, as the years pass,
   we sometimes lose our sense of childlike wonder and fascination,
   becoming worldly-wise or blasé about life,
   taking for granted those things that once stirred our imagination,
   and so sinking into an ever-deeper rut of cynicism and over-familiarity.
Help us to recapture something of the innocence and spontaneity
   of our childhood years:

the ability to look at the world with inquiring eyes,
    to trust in the future
    and to celebrate the present.
Gracious God,
    give us faith in life
    and faith in you,
    through Jesus Christ our Lord.
Amen.

202
Living God,
    we have committed ourselves to the path of discipleship
    and we want to walk it faithfully,
    but we know how easy it is to slip back.
Help us to be alert to dangers,
    able to recognise those things that might trip us up.
Help us to keep our eyes on you,
    knowing that you will lead us safely
    through the pitfalls and obstacles in our path.
And, should we stumble or find ourselves slipping,
    hold on to us,
    keep us steady
    and direct our footsteps
    so that we will find the path once more
    and continue safely on our way
    until our journey's end.
In Christ's name we ask it.
Amen.

203
Lord Jesus Christ,
    you call us,
    as you called your first disciples,
    to follow you:
    not simply to believe,
    nor merely to declare our faith and confess you as Lord,
    but to keep on following wherever you lead.
Help us to follow you faithfully,
    walking wherever you might lead.
Help us to follow your example,
    pursuing the way of love and accepting the road of sacrifice.
Help us to follow through the life of discipleship,
    not allowing ourselves to become distracted,
    nor to lose heart so that we wander away from you,
    but keeping faith to the end.

Lord Jesus Christ,
   you call us,
   as you call all your people,
   to follow you.
Teach us what that means,
   and by your grace help us to respond
   and to be followers of your way,
   to the glory of your name.
Amen.

204
Lord God,
   you know that life isn't always easy.
There are times when we feel exhausted,
   overwhelmed,
   defeated.
Remind us then of those who have gone before us,
   keeping the faith
   and running the race with perseverance.
Remind us of the fellowship we share with all your people,
   and the strength we can gain from one another.
Remind us of our responsibility to those who will come after us,
   the example we need to set to encourage and inspire them.
Above all, remind us of Jesus,
   his willingness to endure the cross for our sake,
   his faithfulness to the end.
So give us strength to battle on,
   faithful in turn,
   in the knowledge that you are waiting to receive us
   and to grant us the joy of your kingdom,
   the prize of everlasting life,
   through Jesus Christ our Lord.
Amen.

205
Lord,
   it's hard,
   faced with disappointment,
   to find new reserves and fresh inspiration to try and try again.
When we've given our all and believe we've achieved something,
   when we've kept on battling despite the obstacles in our way,
   it hurts to accept that there are still more hurdles to face,
   more setbacks to overcome.
Yet though we may sometimes feel weary at the demands,
   we know in our hearts that life is made of such challenges;

that no achievement,
   however special,
   is sufficient to answer all our dreams.
Renew us, then, through your Holy Spirit,
   and give us the faith and commitment we need to walk the pilgrim way,
   pressing on towards the prize you set before us.
Amen.

206
Living God,
   we do not find it easy to journey in faith.
We want a clearer idea of what the future holds,
   a knowledge of where we are heading
   and an explanation of how we are going to get there.
Yet neither life nor faith is like that,
   few things as definite as we would like them to be.
Inspire us, though, by the knowledge that you are journeying with us
   every step of the way.
May that truth equip us with courage to step out into the unknown,
   with faith to follow wherever you lead,
   with trust to walk with humility
   and with commitment to travel on to our journey's end,
   through Jesus Christ our Lord.
Amen.

207
Lord Jesus Christ,
   it is not easy to follow you;
   not if we are serious about discipleship.
You challenge our whole perspective on life,
   calling us not just to a statement of belief but to a way of life.
You are always leading us forward,
   eager to guide us into new experiences of your love
   and a deeper understanding of your purpose,
   yet so often we refuse to follow where you would have us go.
Forgive us for losing the sense of direction
   that marked our early days of discipleship.
Forgive us for trusting you when all goes well
   but doubting the moment life fails to conform to our expectations.
Forgive us for thinking that we have done all that needs to be done,
   imagining that one simple confession of faith suffices for a lifetime.
Lord,
   you are still calling,
   inviting us to respond.
Help us to follow.
Amen.

208
Lord,
    you do not call us to a destination but a journey –
    a journey of continual new discoveries
    and new experiences of your love.
Save us from ever thinking we have arrived;
    from imagining we know all there is to know
    or that we have exhausted the riches of everything you would reveal to us.
Open our eyes to the great adventure of life
    and to the unfathomable mysteries of your purpose,
    and so help us to live as pilgrims,
    travelling in faith as Abraham travelled,
    until we reach at last the kingdom you hold in store for all your people.
Amen.

209
Loving God,
    we thank you for those moments in our lives
    that have been milestones in our journey of faith –
    moments when we have been especially conscious of your presence,
    when faith has grown,
    when truth has dawned on us in an unmistakable way.
We thank you for such times
    but we pray you will help us always to recognise
    that our journey is not ended
    but only just begun.
Teach us that, however many answers we may have,
    there is always more to see,
    more to learn
    and more to understand,
    through Jesus Christ our Lord.
Amen.

Faith

see also Questions of faith

Essentials of faith

210

Lord Jesus Christ,
   we were not there at the stable like the shepherds;
   we were not one of the twelve you chose as your Apostles;
   we were not able to see you heal the sick;
   we were not there as you broke bread in the upper room,
   as they pressed the crown of thorns on your head,
   as you suffered on the cross,
   as you appeared to the disciples following your resurrection,
   as you ascended into heaven.
Yet we can know you as much as any who *were* there,
   for you are with us now,
   with us always,
   here by our sides.
Lord Jesus Christ,
   we thank you for the daily reality of your living presence.
Amen.

211

Loving God,
   we do not know all there is to know,
   or understand all there is to understand,
   but one thing we are sure of:
   that in Jesus Christ we have met with you,
   experiencing your love,
   rejoicing in your mercy,
   receiving your guidance,
   thrilling to your blessing.
There is much still to learn and much that will always be beyond us,
   but we have seen and heard enough to convince us of your grace,
   and we have tasted sufficient of your goodness
   to know that nothing can ever separate us
   from your love revealed in Christ.
Help us to live as he taught us,
   to love as he urged us,
   to serve as he showed us and to trust as he told us.
So may we live in him and he live in us,
   to the glory of your name.
Amen.

212

Gracious God,
    we thank you for the simplicity of the gospel:
    the message of your living, dying and rising among us in Christ.
We thank you that it is not about clever words or subtle concepts,
    but about a concrete expression of your love.
Forgive us for complicating that message:
    for cluttering it up with our ideas and prejudices,
    our attempts to define and delimit,
    our interpretations and terminology.
Open our eyes again to the heart of what it all means
    and, through letting go of so much that is ultimately trivial,
    help us to communicate what really matters:
    the good news of forgiveness
    and new life in Jesus.
We ask it for his sake.
Amen.

213

Lord Jesus Christ,
    we thank you that though we weren't at the stable like the shepherds,
    we can experience new birth in our lives;
    though we weren't able to see you healing the sick,
    we can still be made whole by your touch;
    though we never saw you suffering on the cross,
    nonetheless you died for us;
    though we were not there in the garden as you rose again,
    we can meet you as our risen Lord and Saviour.
For the awesome truth that we can know you as meaningfully today
    as any of those who witnessed your earthly ministry,
    we give you our worship.
Amen.

214

Loving God,
    you call us to live as your people:
    to walk each day by your side,
    seeking your will,
    pursuing what is right,
    and showing your love in our attitudes towards others.
Forgive us that we sometimes make your call so complicated,
    losing sight of the things you really require.
Forgive us that we become preoccupied with the trappings of faith
    rather than focusing on the essentials.

Help us to offer you the sort of life you want to see
    and to be the person you would have us become.
Teach us what you require
    and, by your grace, may we live to the glory of your name,
    through Jesus Christ our Lord.
Amen.

215
Sovereign God,
    we thank you that you took on our humanity,
    walking our earth,
    experiencing our joy and sorrow,
    becoming part of our world of space and time.
We thank you for the experience of those who met with you in Christ,
    and for their testimony to your life-changing power through him.
Above all, we thank you
    that we too can experience that same love and power within our lives;
    that though we may not see Jesus in the flesh
    we can still know him as a living reality in our hearts,
    and so experience for ourselves the good news at the heart of the gospel.
Receive our grateful praise,
    through Jesus Christ our Lord.
Amen.

Faith in action
see also Serving others

216
Lord Jesus Christ,
    we claim to be your followers
    committed to working for your kingdom,
    yet all too often we are reluctant
    to get involved in the needs of our world.
We talk of service
    but are reluctant to roll our sleeves up.
We speak of compassion
    but keep the needy at arm's length.
Teach us not simply to talk of faith
    or speak of love,
    but to show it
    for your name's sake.
Amen.

217

Lord Jesus Christ,
   we proclaim you as our Lord and Saviour,
   we believe you to be God's promised Messiah,
   we preach the gospel of your cross and resurrection.
Yet we so rarely listen to your message:
   your message that challenges and disturbs,
   that calls us to a life of self-denial and sacrifice,
   that speaks of justice for the poor,
   liberty for the imprisoned,
   hope for the oppressed.
Lord Jesus,
   help us to hear not simply what we want to hear,
   but rather what you would say to us.
Amen.

218

Lord Jesus Christ,
   you tell us not to hide our lamp under a bushel basket,
   yet we do it all the time.
Instead of sharing what you have done for us,
   we keep it to ourselves.
Instead of looking to the interests of others,
   we focus on our own.
Instead of reaching out to those in need,
   we shut our minds to their plight.
Repeatedly, our words say one thing
   and our lives another.
Forgive us our failure to honour your calling.
Fill our hearts once more with the joy of knowing you,
   and so may we shine like stars in the world,
   bringing glory to God the Father,
   for your name's sake.
Amen.

219

Lord Jesus Christ,
   we like to think that faith is enough to save us,
   for we know that our deeds are poor
   and our witness is weak,
   incapable in themselves of earning salvation.
We thank you that you see beyond our failures
   to our underlying intentions,
   and that, when we acknowledge our faults,
   you are always willing to have mercy.

Yet save us from using your grace
    as an excuse to abdicate our responsibilities;
    from imagining that the way we live
    and the service we offer
    are unimportant.
Help us to understand that though faith does not depend on works,
    it must show itself through them;
    that the ultimate test of whether our lives are rooted in you
    is whether they bear fruit in your service.
Teach us, then, through the care we offer,
    the love we share
    and the service we give
    to express our commitment to you,
    faith showing itself in action,
    to the glory of your name.
Amen.

220
Gracious God,
    forgive us for those things we should have done but have left undone:
    the acts of kindness we never found time for,
    the thoughtful word never spoken,
    the message of encouragement or concern never sent,
    the helpful deed never attempted.
Forgive us for all the opportunities we have missed:
    the plans we never made,
    the dreams we never brought to reality,
    the possibilities we never even imagined,
    the gifts we never used.
Forgive us for our failure to serve you as we promised:
    the prayers we never offered,
    the sacrifices we never made,
    the faith we never had,
    and the commitment we never gave.
Forgive us for so often having time only for self:
    for being self-centred,
    self-important,
    self-righteous,
    self-interested,
    self-indulgent,
    self-opinionated.
Forgive us for forgetting our friends,
    our neighbours,
    and, above all, you.

Gracious God,
    save us from being people of unfulfilled intentions.
Help us to translate our thoughts into actions,
        to put our preaching into practice,
        and to turn our good intentions into good deeds,
        to the glory of your name.
Amen.

221

Gracious God,
    we do not know you or serve you as we should,
    our faith sometimes short both on theory and practice.
We are careless in making time for you,
    rarely stopping to read your word or seek your will.
We are casual in discipleship,
    more concerned with serving ourselves than you or others.
Help us to know you better and to love you more deeply,
        and may that in turn help us to prove our love for you in action,
        showing the sincerity of our faith by practising what we preach,
        to the glory of your name.
Amen.

222

Living God,
    too easily we turn faith into a matter of personal devotion and fulfilment,
    forgetting that it must show itself in the way we live.
We make time for prayer and worship,
    we read and study your word,
    but then we fail to go out into the world
    and make real there the truth of what we believe.
Forgive us,
    and help us to minister in your name,
    bringing peace, hope, help and healing,
    sharing your love
    and working to bring your kingdom closer here on earth.
In the name of Christ we ask it.
Amen.

223

Sovereign God,
    you tell us that from those who have been given much,
    much will be expected in turn.
Forgive us for forgetting sometimes the second part of that challenge,
    rejoicing in your goodness,
    celebrating your gift of life and the new life you offer in Christ,

but forgetting that all this brings responsibility as well as privilege,
and that one day we will be called to account
for the way we have lived and acted.
Teach us, then, to live wisely,
   responding to your guidance
   and doing your will,
   even though, in this life, everything may seem to count against it.
Help us to be faithful to you,
   as you are faithful to us,
   through Jesus Christ our Lord,
   Amen.

224

Lord Jesus Christ,
   we have been guilty of focusing on individual blessing
   at the cost of corporate responsibility,
   more concerned with what we will receive from you
   than with what we should give to others.
Forgive us for turning the gospel on its head,
   tailoring it to suit our own ends
   rather than allowing it to shape our lives.
Forgive us for being so preoccupied with heaven
   that we forget needs here on earth.
Teach us that, though we can never earn our salvation,
   we need to show the reality of our faith through the way we live.
Show us where you would have us serve,
   and help us to love you as you love all,
   for your name's sake.
Amen.

225

Lord Jesus Christ,
   help us to show our faith not just in abstract love for the world
   but also in practical service to those around us.
In our daily relationships –
   at home,
   at work,
   at leisure,
   at church;
   whenever and wherever it might be –
   teach us to live out our faith in such a way
   that our lives embody the claims and truth of the gospel,
   to the glory of your name.
Amen.

226
Lord Jesus Christ,
   we like to think we have founded our lives firmly upon you,
   but the reality may not be as we imagine.
Though we declare our faith and profess your name,
   though we talk of commitment and speak of service,
   there is a danger of this being all show and no substance,
   a matter of words rather than deeds.
We fail to listen to what you would tell us,
   we are slow to reflect on what discipleship really means,
   and we offer you only a part of our lives,
   keeping the rest back for fear of what you might ask of us.
Like the foolish builder,
   we hear your words but do not act upon them,
   our good intentions never translated into action.
Forgive us,
   despite your guidance,
   for building our lives on sand rather than rock.
Open our ears,
   our minds and our hearts,
   so that we may not only hear what you would say to us
   but also respond with body, mind and soul,
   to the glory of your name.
Amen.

227
Lord,
   it's easy to go to church,
   hard to reach out to the world.
It's easy to say our prayers,
   hard to act upon them.
It's easy to offer our money,
   hard to give you our lives.
It's easy to sing your praises,
   hard to live to your glory.
Forgive us for so often taking the easy way,
   the way of outward show rather than inner faith.
Move within us,
   so that the words of our lips may show themselves
   in the thoughts of our hearts,
   and the claims of our faith may be proven
   through the sincerity of our service.
Amen.

228

Lord,
  we are good at talking about faith,
  at making the right noises and saying the right words.
We are not bad either at looking the part –
  turning up at church,
  looking respectable,
  getting involved in Christian activities.
Yet when it comes to living the faith,
  so often our lives show too much of us
  and too little of you.
Forgive us when the things we say and do
  deny rather than affirm the gospel;
  when we conceal our discipleship
  for fear of what others may think.
Help us to follow you faithfully,
  reflecting your love,
  demonstrating your compassion
  and responding to your guidance.
Touch our hearts
  and strengthen our faith,
  so that in the days ahead we may live and work for you,
  and bring glory to your holy name.
Amen.

229

Loving God,
  through Christ you demonstrated the wonder of your grace,
  living among us,
  sharing our humanity
  and giving freely of yourself.
You didn't just speak of love;
  you showed it in action.
Forgive us for so rarely doing the same,
  our lives belying instead of reinforcing our words.
We talk of forgiving others, yet we nurse grievances;
  of being content, yet we are full of envy;
  of serving others, yet we serve self;
  of loving truth, yet we deal falsely.
We speak of commitment, but we are careless in discipleship;
  of faith, but we are full of doubt;
  of vision, but we are narrow in our outlook;
  of being a new creation, but we continue in just the same way as before.
Forgive us and help us not simply to talk about faith
  but to demonstrate it through the people we are.

Grant that our words and our deeds may be one,
    so that we may witness effectively to your renewing, redeeming power,
    through Jesus Christ our Lord.
Amen.

Growing and continuing in faith
see also Discipleship, journey of; Maturity in Christ, growth in

230
Loving God,
    once more we come to worship you,
    not out of tradition or duty,
    but because we want to remember,
    to learn,
    and to understand.
For all our faith,
    all our desire to serve you,
    we are conscious of how weak our discipleship has been,
    and we hunger to know you better,
    to grasp more fully the love you have shown in Christ,
    and to live more in tune with the example he has shown.
Meet with us, we pray.
May your word of old come to life,
    the message we have heard so often speak with new power.
Come now, and work within us,
    that we in turn may work for you,
    through Jesus Christ our Lord.
Amen.

231
Gracious God,
    we thank you for your gracious invitation in Christ
    to know your love
    and share your life.
We praise you for coming in him,
    so that we can come to you.
Teach us that we need to go on making our response day after day;
    that it is not a one-off thing,
    once done and then forgotten,
    but an ongoing renewal of commitment,
    a consecrating to you of all we are and all we do.
So, once more, we bring you our worship,
    we offer you our service

and we dedicate our lives,
  in Jesus' name.
Amen.

232
Living God,
  we thank you that you provide us not only with daily bread
  but also with the bread of life –
  inner nourishment that means we need never go spiritually hungry again.
You offer us so much through which to nourish our faith:
  your love in Christ,
  the inner presence of your Holy Spirit,
  and the testimony of the scriptures –
  and yet all too often we fail to feed ourselves as we should.
The result is that we grow weak instead of strong,
  our faith starved,
  emaciated,
  wasting away –
  a pale shadow of what it ought to be.
Forgive us,
  and teach us to nurture our faith
  so that we may be strong in your service,
  to your glory.
Amen.

233
Lord Jesus Christ,
  you know that we want to follow you,
  but you know also how hard we find it to do so.
Despite our good intentions,
  we repeatedly slip back into our old ways,
  pursuing our own ends rather than your will.
Instead of working and witnessing for you,
  we are lukewarm in service and weak in discipleship.
Instead of growing,
  our faith has become stale and tired,
  no longer challenging or inspiring us
  as in the days when we first believed.
Forgive us for falling away so easily.
Cleanse, renew and restore us by your redeeming touch,
  and help us to live for you today, tomorrow and every day,
  sure and steadfast,
  to the glory of your name.
Amen.

234
Loving God,
  occasionally there are moments that we never want to end,
  moments so special that we wish time would stand still
  so that we could hold on to them for ever,
  but we know that life and faith are not like that,
  instead always needing to move on if they are not to grow stale.
Help us, then, to be open to new experiences of your love
  new insights into your greatness,
  new responses to your call,
  and a new awareness of your guidance,
  so that we may know you better each day,
  until that time we rejoice in your presence for all eternity,
  in the joy of Christ that will never fade or perish.
In his name we ask it.
Amen.

235
Lord Jesus Christ,
  we remember your words to the disciples
  that the kingdom of heaven belongs to little children,
  and we remember also your warning that unless we become like children
  we can never hope to enter that kingdom.
Teach us what that means.
Grant us the childlike qualities we need to grow in faith –
  a child's innocence and hunger to learn,
  a child's love and total trust.
Help us,
  like them,
  to step out gladly into the great adventure of faith,
  to the glory of your name.
Amen.

Faithfulness of God

see also Greatness and wonder of God; Praise and thanksgiving;
Strength in weakness; Trust; Will and purpose of God

236
Almighty God,
    teach us to remember all you have done
    and to give you the praise you deserve.
Teach us each day to recall your creative acts,
    your mighty deeds throughout history,
    and your faithful dealings with your people across the years.
Above all, teach us to remember your graciousness in Jesus Christ –
    your coming, living, dying and rising among us,
    so that we might have life in all its fullness.
For the memory of such things,
    and the constant reminder of them we receive each day,
    we give you our thanks and praise,
    through Jesus Christ our Lord.
Amen.

237
Almighty God,
    we remember again all you have done across the years:
    your creative acts,
    your mighty deeds throughout history,
    your gift of Jesus Christ.
We remember all you have done for us:
    your sovereign love,
    your gracious mercy
    and your constant guidance every day of our lives.
Forgive us that so often and so easily we forget those things,
    brooding instead over our troubles,
    coveting what we do not have,
    preoccupied with our personal well-being rather than your kingdom.
Help us each day to remind ourselves of your goodness,
    to recall the ways you have blessed us,
    and so to keep you at the forefront of our lives,
    living and working for your glory.
In Christ's name we ask it.
Amen.

238
God of truth, justice and power,
    we praise you that you are also a God of love.

Though we disobey your commandments
   and lose sight of your goodness,
      though we fail to love others and are forgetful of you,
      still you love us.
Though we reject your guidance,
   betray our convictions
   and deny our calling,
      still you care.
Always you are there,
   watching over us,
   calling us back,
   welcoming us home.
Day after day we receive new blessings, mercy and strength
   from your loving hands.
Gracious God,
   we praise you for your awesome love and your great faithfulness,
   in the name of Christ.
Amen.

239
Gracious God,
   we thank you for the many ways you provide for us,
   the love you so faithfully show
   and the blessings you give beyond our deserving.
Forgive us for taking your goodness for granted
   instead of appreciating it as we should.
Forgive us for failing to trust you despite all you have done,
   trusting instead in other people or other things.
Teach us to put our faith in you,
   knowing that whatever we may be up against
   you will provide the help we need to face it,
   through Jesus Christ our Lord.
Amen.

240
Gracious God,
   we thank you that you are here by our side,
   wanting to meet us,
   greet us
   and teach us.
We thank you for being with us everywhere –
   at every moment,
   every place and every occasion –
   watching over us as a father watches over his child.
Day by day,
   you stay close –

recognised or unrecognised,
remembered or forgotten,
obeyed or disobeyed,
acknowledged or taken for granted.
Though our response to you is varied and our commitment wavering,
you are always the same:
ever-faithful,
all-loving,
always true.
We have no way of knowing what the future may hold,
whether for good or ill,
but what we do know,
and hold on to,
is that you will remain the same,
always there when we need you,
and that nothing finally can ever separate us
from your love in Christ.
For that assurance,
receive our praise,
in his name.
Amen.

241
Living God,
help us to remember that you are a God who never sleeps,
a God on whom we can depend in any and every situation.
When we feel lost and alone,
teach us that you are there.
When we feel overwhelmed by trouble,
unsure of our ability to get through,
help us to remember that you are close by.
When we feel uncertain of the way ahead,
fearful of what the future may hold,
teach us that you are watching over us.
Help us to understand that, whatever we may face,
you will guide and guard us,
protecting us from evil
and enfolding us in your everlasting arms,
and in that knowledge may we meet every day with quiet trust
and glad thanksgiving,
in Christ's name.
Amen.

242
Lord Jesus Christ,
thank you for the way you watch over us throughout our lives,

the way you are continually there to guard and guide us,
    whatever we may face.
When we wander far from your side,
    you do not abandon us to our fate but instead come looking for us,
    your love refusing to let us go.
Though we may forsake you,
    you never forsake us.
Though we are faithless,
    you remain faithful.
We praise you for that great truth,
    and we ask forgiveness for the areas in our lives
    in which we continue to go astray.
Help us to follow you more closely in the days ahead,
    to the glory of your name.
Amen.

243
Loving God,
    thank you for this day and all the opportunities it brings:
    moments to work and rest,
    to give and receive,
    to wonder and worship.
Thank you for having been with us throughout our lives –
    always there to guide our footsteps and lead us forward.
Thank you for the assurance of your continuing guidance –
    the knowledge that whatever the future may bring,
    whatever challenges we may face or trials we may endure,
    you will be there to see us through,
    giving us the strength and resources we need,
    and a joy that cannot be shaken.
God of past, present and future,
    the same yesterday, today and tomorrow,
    we praise you for each and every moment,
    and consecrate them all to your service.
We ask it in the name of Christ.
Amen.

244
Loving God,
    we know we shouldn't be afraid but sometimes we are –
    afraid of what the future might hold
    and whether we will have the strength to meet it.
Thank you for the assurance that whatever we may face,
    you will be there beside us.

Thank you for your promise to lift us up and help us to start again,
    however often we may fail.
Thank you for the times you have reached out in the past,
    the experiences we can look back on
    when your arms have been there to support us
    when we needed them most.
Teach us to trust you more completely
    and so to step out in faith,
    confident that, though we may stumble,
    you will set us on our feet once more.
Amen.

245
Loving God,
    we thank you for all the ways you are with us
    and all the ways you grant your blessing.
We thank you for the guidance you give,
    the strength you supply,
    the mercy you show
    and the love with which you surround us.
We thank you that your purpose extends beyond this life into eternity;
    that you are holding the best in store.
Teach us to walk with you each day
    knowing you are always by our side,
    and so may we trust you for the future,
    secure in the everlasting hope you have given us in Christ,
    that nothing shall ever destroy.
Amen.

246
Loving God,
    we thank you that you are a God we can depend on,
    a God in whom we can put our trust.
What you promise is done;
    what you purpose is fulfilled.
We remember your promise to Abraham –
    that, through his offspring, all the world would be blessed;
    to Moses –
    that you would lead the Israelites out of Egypt;
    to Isaiah –
    that you would deliver your people from exile;
    to your prophets –
    that the Messiah would come;
    to the Apostles –
    that he would rise again on the third day.

We thank you that you fulfilled those promises,
    just as you said you would –
    your Son born from the line of Abraham,
    your chosen nation set free from slavery,
    your people returning joyfully to Jerusalem,
    your promised deliverer born in Bethlehem,
    your power seen in the resurrection of Christ.
We thank you for what that means for us today –
    that we can live each moment with confidence,
    whatever our circumstances may be,
    whatever times of testing may befall us,
    knowing that, though all else may fail,
    you will not;
    though heaven and earth may pass away,
    your words will endure for ever.
So we look forward to that day when your purpose is fulfilled
    and you are all in all.
Until then, we will trust in you,
    secure in your love,
    confident in your eternal purpose,
    assured that your will shall be done.
Receive our thanks,
    in the name of Christ.
Amen.

247
Sovereign God,
    we thank you for the way you are at work in our lives,
    constantly looking to refashion us in your image.
We praise you that, despite our lack of faith,
    our many faults
    and our sometimes wilful disobedience,
    you never give up,
    patiently looking to recreate us
    through the power of your Holy Spirit.
Come to us now in all our weakness,
    and by your grace,
    renew, redeem and restore us in the likeness of Christ,
    for his name's sake.
Amen.

_____ Fulfilment, true nature of _____

248
Eternal God,
    in a world of constant flux we thank you that you remain the same –
    solid,
    unchanging,
    dependable –
    a God in whom we can put our trust.
Though all else fails,
    you will not.
Though empires come and go,
    your kingdom will endure for ever.
Teach us to base our lives on that fact,
    celebrating the many blessings you give us now
    but recognising also where our eternal fulfilment lies.
So may we rejoice in the light of your love,
    today, tomorrow and always.
Amen.

249
Gracious God,
    forgive us the greed within us that spoils and destroys,
    always looking for more instead of being content with what we have.
Forgive us for being obsessed with instant satisfaction and material gain,
    for becoming sensitised to the spirit of this age
    and allowing ourselves to lose sight of
    the things in life that can really satisfy.
Teach us to hunger and thirst instead for the things of your kingdom.
So shall we discover not just how much we have to be thankful for now
    but also the treasures in heaven that only you can give.
In Christ's name we pray.
Amen.

250
Living God,
    we like to imagine that possessions are not important to us
    but the reality is different.
We surround ourselves with all kinds of belongings
    and we are constantly seeking more.
Some contribute much to our lives,
    others yield nothing,
    but all of them can so easily keep us from you,
    closing our eyes to what is ultimately important in life.

Forgive us the time, money and resources we waste
　　in accumulating what we do not need.
Forgive the selfishness
　　and the wasted opportunities to give to or serve others
　　that all this entails.
Teach us to travel light,
　　recognising where true fulfilment lies,
　　and so may our service be deepened
　　and our relationship with you enriched,
　　through the grace of Jesus Christ.
Amen.

251
Living God,
　　you have taught us that we should long to know you better:
　　not just to want that
　　but to urgently, passionately and wholeheartedly yearn for it,
　　striving with all our being to understand your will
　　and fulfil your purpose.
You have told us that those who hunger and thirst after righteousness
　　shall be filled.
Teach us the secret of such hunger.
Instead of cluttering our lives with so much that can never satisfy,
　　teach us to empty ourselves so that we may be filled by you;
　　to desire your kingdom,
　　seek your will
　　and study your word,
　　earnestly,
　　eagerly,
　　expectantly.
However much we know of your love,
　　however richly you may have blessed us,
　　teach us to keep that hunger alive,
　　to thirst always for a deepening of our faith,
　　a strengthening of our service
　　and a greater awareness of your purpose,
　　through Jesus Christ our Lord.
Amen.

252
Lord Jesus Christ,
　　we have no need to be thirsty,
　　for we have tasted the living water you offer
　　and experienced first-hand its power to satisfy,
　　yet sometimes we turn our back on the life-giving spring you offer.

We seek fulfilment elsewhere –
   in money,
   material possessions,
   work,
   friendships –
   forgetting that none of these,
   however much pleasure they may bring,
   can meet our deepest needs.
Help us to enjoy the blessings you have given,
   the innumerable good things in life,
   but help us also to keep a proper sense of perspective,
   recognising that you are the one who gives meaning to all.
So may the water of life well up within us
   and overflow in joyful praise,
   loving service
   and spontaneous witness,
   to the glory of your name.
Amen.

253
Lord Jesus Christ,
   we know that true riches do not lie on earth
   and yet we find it hard truly to accept that fact.
Day after day,
   we strive to put a bit of extra money into our pocket,
   and we yearn to splash out a little,
   to treat ourselves to those few extra luxuries,
   to afford our dream holiday, new car or luxury home.
We find it hard to see beyond the alluring pleasures of this material world,
   even though we know that so much of what it seems to offer is illusory,
   unable to satisfy for more than a few moments,
   let alone to meet our deepest needs.
Open our eyes to true riches:
   to the blessings you have given us
   and to all that you yet hold in store.
Help us to appreciate the joy and fulfilment that you alone can offer,
   and to celebrate the inheritance beyond price
   that comes through knowing and serving you.
We ask it in your name.
Amen.

254
Eternal God,
   we spend so much of our lives seeking happiness,
   yet much of the time we are frustrated.

We turn from one thing to another,
    believing for a moment that it may offer the fulfilment we crave,
    but so many pleasures are fleeting,
    here today and gone tomorrow.
There are times when life seems empty,
    when nothing seems permanent,
    not even those things most precious to us.
Help us to find the rest for our souls that you alone can give;
    to discover in you that inner peace which can never change
    but which will go on satisfying for all eternity.
Help us to live each day in tune with you,
    rejoicing in all you have given
    and anticipating all you have yet to give,
    through Christ our Lord.
Amen.

255
Gracious God,
    we know we can never repay the love you have shown us,
    but we long to show our gratitude by loving you in return,
    by serving you as you desire,
    by being the sort of people you call us to be.
Set us free from our preoccupation with the things of this world,
    from our obsession with self,
    from the pride, greed and envy
    which blind us to all that really matters.
Teach us to live according to the values of your kingdom,
    where it is in giving that we shall receive,
    in letting go that we shall find,
    in being poor that we shall become rich.
Take us and use us, by your grace,
    through Jesus Christ our Lord.
Amen.

256
Loving God,
    thank you for your great gift of life in all its fullness –
    everything you have given to enjoy,
    celebrate and live for.
Thank you for the innumerable blessings you shower upon us every day:
    love to share,
    beauty to enthral,
    health to enjoy,
    food to eat and so much more –
    a world to excite, fascinate and savour.

Above all, thank you for the life you have given us in Christ;
    a life that you want us and all people to enjoy
    not just now but for all eternity.
Teach us to celebrate your love in all its richness,
    to rejoice in your gifts in all their abundance
    and to celebrate life in all its fullness,
    to the glory of your name.
Amen.

257
Living God,
    we have so much to celebrate,
    more than previous generations would have imagined possible,
    yet it does not bring us peace.
We still worry about the future and brood over the past;
    still fret over money, work or loved ones,
    and still wrestle with pressures, fears, anxieties and questions.
For all their sophistication and ingenuity,
    the technology and wealth of modern society cannot meet
    our deepest needs,
    nor calm the storm within.
So we come to you who alone can nourish our souls
    and renew our being –
    the one in whom we find not the extras of life but life itself.
Teach us to measure all else against who and what you are,
    and, in getting that into perspective,
    may we discover the peace you promise to all who know you,
    through Jesus Christ our Lord.
Amen.

_____ Greatness and wonder of God _____

see also Faithfulness of God; Praise and thanksgiving;
Strength in weakness

258

Almighty and everlasting God,
 with awe and wonder we come to worship you.
You are higher than our highest thoughts
 but always close by our side;
 greater than we can ever imagine
 yet made known to us in Christ;
 all powerful
 but nurturing us as a mother tends her child;
 constantly at work in human history
 yet having a special concern for every one of us.
Though we stretch imagination to the limit
 we barely begin to glimpse how wonderful you are.
Though you sometimes seem distant,
 always you are near.
Almighty and everlasting God,
 give us humility to acknowledge our weakness beside your greatness,
 faith to trust in you despite our doubts,
 joy in knowing you despite the limitations of our understanding,
 and peace in serving you,
 knowing that you are the Lord of all,
 a God both near and far.
In Christ's name we ask it.
Amen.

259

Almighty God,
 we will never grasp the whole truth about you,
 nor even a fraction of it,
 but what we do see, when we take time to look,
 is enough still to fill us with awe and wonder.
You are the Lord of all,
 the Creator of the ends of the earth,
 the giver and sustainer of life.
You are all good,
 all loving,
 all merciful,
 involved in every moment of every day.
Forgive us that we sometimes take that for granted,

our hearts no longer thrilling as they once did
to the majesty of your presence.
Forgive us for growing so accustomed to you
that we become casual, almost blasé, in our relationship,
losing our sense of reverence as we come to worship you.
Open our eyes afresh to your greatness,
your power,
your sovereignty over all.
Give us again a glimpse of your glory,
through Jesus Christ our Lord.
Amen.

260

Almighty and most wonderful God,
unsearchable and inexhaustible,
greater than we can ever imagine,
higher than our highest thoughts,
enthroned in glory and splendour,
we offer again our worship,
recognising that your ways are not our ways,
nor your thoughts our thoughts.
Forgive us for forgetting that sometimes,
imagining that we know all there is to know about you.
Forgive us our narrow vision and closed minds,
the way we have tied you down to our own understanding,
closing our hearts to anything that challenges our restricted horizons,
and so losing sight of your greatness.
Remind us that you have always more to say,
more to reveal and more to do.
Open our eyes, minds and hearts to who and what you are,
and so fill us with awe and wonder,
joy and thanksgiving,
praise and worship,
now and for evermore.
Amen.

261

Almighty God,
you have done more for us than we can ever begin to acknowledge.
You have done so much throughout history,
more than words can ever fully express.
So we come once more in grateful and heartfelt worship.
We praise you for the wonder of the universe,
the loveliness of the world,
and the beauty of your creation.

We thank you for the joy of life,
   with all there is to delight, fascinate, challenge and enrich.
We rejoice in the new life you have given us in Christ –
   the hope, strength, peace and inspiration
   you grant us each day through him.
We praise you for the constancy of your love,
   the breadth of your purpose
   and the awesome extent of your mercy.
You have blessed us beyond our deserving,
   showering us with good things,
   and yet you still hold the best in store.
Almighty God,
   for your mighty acts and sovereign deeds,
   we give you our worship and offer you our lives in glad response,
   through Jesus Christ our Lord.
Amen.

262
Eternal God,
   mighty and mysterious,
   sovereign over all,
   it is beyond the power of human words to express your greatness,
   for you are higher than we can ever begin to imagine.
We praise you for that truth,
   yet we confess, also, that it can be hard to live with,
   for it can make you seem remote,
   distant,
   detached from our situation,
   oblivious to our need.
We thank you that such times are rare,
   but they do come –
   times when you seem so mysterious,
   so far removed from our situation,
   that we question whether you are there at all.
We seek,
   yet we do not find;
   we ask,
   but we do not receive;
   we cry out for help,
   but you do not answer.
Help us in such moments
   to gain inspiration from those who have felt the same before us,
   yet who have emerged from the darkness
   to find that you have been there all along,
   leading them by the hand even when they could not see it.

Assure us of your continuing purpose,
    your enduring love and your final triumph,
    through Jesus Christ our Lord.
Amen.

263
Gracious God,
    you are above all,
    beneath all,
    beyond all,
    within all.
You are God of past, present and future;
    of space and time,
    heaven and earth;
    of all people, all creatures and all creation.
Forgive us for sometimes losing sight of those awesome realities,
    settling instead for a fragmented picture of who you are
    shaped by our narrow horizons
    and our flawed and limited understanding.
Stir our imagination,
    and help us to see a little more clearly each day
    the wonder of your glory.
In Christ's name we ask it.
Amen.

264
Great and wonderful God,
    with awe and amazement we worship you,
    for you are greater than our minds can fathom,
    beyond our highest thoughts,
    sovereign over all.
We worship you in your holiness,
    and yet we also greet you as a friend,
    for you have shared our humanity,
    identifying yourself wholly with our world
    and demonstrating the awesome extent of your love.
You have broken down the barriers that keep us apart,
    and so we know you with us day by day –
    constantly by our side.
Great and wonderful God,
    give us a sense of your greatness and your grace,
    your power and your gentleness,
    your otherness and your nearness.
Remind us each day that your eternal purpose spans all creation
    yet includes our lives, here and now.

So may we give you glory,
    through Jesus Christ our Lord.
Amen.

265
Living God,
    thank you for everything that speaks of your loving purpose;
    all the ways you teach, guide and challenge,
    calling us forward in faith.
Forgive us that we sometimes lose sight
    of the great things you have done
    and the wonders you have yet to reveal.
Draw near in love,
    and open our hearts to all the ways you are at work,
    our eyes to your glory all around us,
    our ears to your living word,
    and our minds to your truth.
So may we grasp each day a little more of who and what you are,
    acknowledging your greatness,
    marvelling at your love,
    rejoicing in your blessings
    and celebrating your inexhaustible mercy,
    through Jesus Christ our Lord.
Amen.

266
Living God,
    we know that your ways are not our ways,
    or your thoughts our thoughts.
We know that you are sovereign over heaven and earth,
    ruler over space and time –
    above,
    beyond,
    before
    and after all.
Yet you have made yourself known to us in Christ,
    revealing your love,
    demonstrating your mercy,
    granting your blessing
    and sharing your life.
In him,
    we glimpse something of your majesty
    and experience the wonder of your grace.

From him,
>   we receive peace and fulfilment that passes all understanding.

Through him,
>   we offer our thanks
>   and give to you honour and worship,
>   praise and glory,
>   now and for evermore.

Amen.

267

Omnipotent God,
>   you are able to do more in our lives
>   than we can ever begin to imagine.

Forgive us for losing sight of that fact –
>   for being content to muddle along,
>   frustrating your will
>   and quenching your Spirit through the narrowness of our vision.

Give us today a new sense of all you want to achieve
>   and the many ways you are able to use us
>   in achieving your purpose.

Stir our imagination
>   and send us out renewed in faith
>   to live and work for your glory,
>   through Jesus Christ our Lord.

Amen.

268

Sovereign God,
>   all too often we lose sight of your greatness,
>   settling instead for a picture of you we feel comfortable with.

We have frustrated your will through the smallness of our vision.

We have missed opportunities to serve you
>   through the narrowness of our horizons.

We have denied ourselves your mercy
>   through the confines we place upon your grace.

Repeatedly we have presumed that your ways are our ways
>   and your thoughts our thoughts,
>   forgetting that you are beyond words or human understanding.

Forgive us,
>   and teach us never to underestimate the awesomeness of your being
>   or the extent of your love.

Amen.

269

Sovereign God,
> you are the Creator of all,
> the Lord of history,
> ruler over space and time.

You are greater than our minds can fathom,
> your ways unlike ours,
> and your thoughts so very different to our own.

You alone deserve praise and worship.

Yet all too often,
> without realising it,
> we pay homage to other gods,
> idols of material wealth and worldly satisfaction
> that have no power to satisfy.

Forgive us for our folly,
> for inadvertently bringing you down to our level
> and losing sight of who you are.

Help us to open our lives to your living and searching presence,
> and so may we honour you in all we are and all we do.

Amen.

Guidance

see also Call of God; Will and purpose of God

270

Living God,
   time and again we ask you to speak to us,
   to reveal your will and give us your guidance,
   but all too often when your call comes we fail to recognise it.
Though we talk of prayer being a two-way encounter,
   the reality is usually different;
   we seldom seriously expect to hear your voice.
Give us a readiness to be guided by the wisdom of others
   so that we may recognise your voice
   and understand what you are saying.
We ask it in the name of Christ.
Amen.

271

Living God,
   you do not compel us to serve you
   but you invite us rather to respond to your love.
You do not impose your will upon us
   or dictate the course we should take,
   but instead you offer your guidance,
   giving us signposts to walk by,
   yet ultimately leaving the decisions we must make in our hands.
We thank you for this wonderful expression of trust,
   this freedom to choose and discover for ourselves,
   and we ask that you will help us to use it wisely,
   trusting you in return,
   and seeking, so far as we understand it,
   to honour your will.
Give us wisdom and courage to make the right decisions,
   at the right time
   and in the right place,
   to the glory of your name.
Amen.

272

Lord Jesus Christ,
   we praise you for your willingness to share our humanity,
   and for everything that means.

We thank you that you endured the darkness of death,
    knowingly offering your life.
We rejoice that you rose again,
    and that you were present once more,
    leading the way to life in all its fullness.
Teach us that, whatever we may face, you will guide our footsteps,
    showing us the path we must take
    and leading us safely towards your kingdom.
Lord Jesus Christ,
    we praise you for that assurance,
    and we put our trust in you,
    this day and always.
Amen.

273
Sovereign God,
    we cannot always make sense of life,
    your purpose sometimes hard to understand
    and our experiences a puzzle.
We feel frustrated when things don't work out as we hope;
    confused when the way we thought you were leading us
    no longer feels right;
    troubled when doors that once had beckoned
    suddenly seem closed firmly in our face.
We cannot be sure whether such moments are meant to happen
    or whether they run counter to your purpose,
    but what we know for certain is that where one door closes
    you are able to open another.
Help us, instead of regretting what has been,
    to look forward to what is to come
    and to be ready to grasp the future,
    responding to each opportunity you give us as it comes.
In the name of Christ we ask it.
Amen.

Hope and despair

see also Adversity, faith in; Intercession: For those who mourn;
Kingdom of God; New beginnings: Resurrection hope;
Trust; Will and purpose of God

274
Almighty God,
  we find it hard sometimes not to despair of our world.
When we look at its pain and suffering,
  sorrow and despair,
  hatred and division,
  evil and injustice,
  we fear for the future,
  and struggle to make sense of it all.
Yet we remember today that you too feel sorrow,
  more than we can ever begin to imagine.
Unlike us, though, you never give up –
  your love willing to give everything,
  even your only Son,
  to redeem, restore and renew.
Inspire us through that knowledge,
  and so may we continue to strive for the coming of your kingdom,
  until that day when all things are reconciled to you in Christ,
  and we are one with you and him,
  now and for evermore.
Amen.

275
Gracious God,
  there are times when we find ourselves
  in the wilderness of doubt and despair.
We look at our lives,
  at the world,
  even at you,
  and we are overwhelmed by a sense of hopelessness,
  by questions as to why you do not act to establish your kingdom
  or respond to us in our time of need.
Help us at such moments, when all seems dark,
  to put our faith in you,
  trusting that your light will finally shine again.
Inspire us with the knowledge that, time and again,
  it has been in the wilderness experiences of people's lives
  that you have been supremely at work –

challenging,
deepening
and strengthening their faith,
equipping them for new avenues of service,
and opening the way to a richer experience of your love.
In that assurance,
lead us forward,
through Jesus Christ our Lord.
Amen.

276

Loving God,
we thank you for all those times when you have come to our aid,
just when we have begun to lose hope.
We face problems and difficulties to which we see no solution,
only for you to give us guidance when we need it most.
We feel hopelessly alone,
only to discover you by our side.
We wrestle with sorrow and despair,
only for your light to break into the darkness,
bringing joy and hope through the knowledge of your love.
Teach us, through such experiences,
to remember that, however bleak a moment may seem,
you will never abandon or forsake us,
and in that confidence may we live each day,
through Jesus Christ our Lord.
Amen.

277

Father God,
so often in life we find that after joy comes sorrow,
after laughter, tears,
after pleasure, pain.
Deep down we know that we cannot have one without the other.
But sometimes when life is dark we find that hard to accept,
even wishing we experienced no joy at all
if it would save us pain afterwards.
Yet you were present equally, Father,
in the joy of Jesus' birth
and the sorrow of his death.
Teach us, then, to live with both the good
and the bad,
the times of celebration
and the times of despair,
realising that, though we may not see it,
you are present in each of them,

working to bringing new beginnings,
new hope,
whether in this life or the life to come.
In the name of Christ, we praise you.
Amen.

278
Gracious God,
   as the years pass,
   so our energy and enthusiasm for life can pass with them.
Though some of our goals are realised,
   many are not and probably never will be,
   and the idealism of our youth is all too easily replaced
   by a world-weary cynicism,
   such that, instead of eagerly anticipating the future,
   we are content simply to get by,
   drifting from one day to the next.
Yet, in Christ, you have given a hope that never fades
   and a purpose that endures for ever,
   opening up a life of infinite possibilities
   and constant new beginnings.
Open our eyes to that wonderful truth,
   and so, whatever hopes may be dashed or goals thwarted,
   may we continue always to travel in faith,
   looking forward to that day when your kingdom shall come
   and your will be done,
   in the name of Christ.
Amen.

279
Gracious God,
   we thank you that you are always with us,
   in the bad times as well as the good,
   the difficult as well as the easy,
   the sad as well as the happy.
We thank you that
   though we have sometimes been unsure of the way ahead,
   you have always been there to guide us;
   though we have felt discouraged,
   you have offered us fresh inspiration;
   though we have been in despair,
   yet you have given us hope.
Through all the changing circumstances of life,
   we have found from personal experience
   that your steadfast love never ceases
   and that your mercies are new every morning.

May the knowledge of all you have done
   give us confidence in the days ahead,
   so that whatever problems we face,
   whatever disappointments we experience,
   whatever sorrows may befall us,
   we will still find reason to look forward,
   reason to believe in the future
   and reason to hope.
Lord of all hopefulness,
   hear our prayer,
   in the name of Christ.
Amen.

280

Living God,
   we praise you for the promise
   that nothing can ever overcome your light.
We thank you that even when life seems dark and hopeless,
   when we search but cannot glimpse your presence
   and call yet cannot hear your voice,
   still you are with us,
   the fire of your love inexorably burning off the clouds
   until the sun breaks through once again,
   bathing us in its light.
May that knowledge sustain us through the bleakest moments,
   bringing the assurance that good will triumph over evil,
   hope replace despair,
   joy come after sorrow,
   and life triumph over death –
   even the darkest night turned to day.
All this we ask through Jesus Christ our Lord.
Amen.

281

Lord,
   it is hard sometimes not to lose faith in your purpose.
When hopes are dashed,
   when dreams are shattered,
   when one disappointment piles up on another,
   it's difficult not to lose heart completely,
   not to retreat into a shell of despair.
We want to believe we can change,
   but there seems little evidence to support it.
We want to believe the world can be different,
   but experience appears to prove otherwise.

Our hearts tells us one thing,
  our head says another,
  and the latter finally wins the day.
Yet you have promised that nothing in heaven or on earth
  will finally overcome your purpose,
  and throughout history you have shown that to be true,
  constantly overturning human expectations,
  hope returning like a phoenix from the ashes.
Speak to us now through the faith and vision of those who have gone before,
  so that, however dark the world may seem,
  we too may dare to hope in turn,
  through Jesus Christ our Lord.
Amen.

282

Loving God,
  so many things in life have promised much but delivered little.
We have set ourselves targets but failed to hit them.
We have achieved goals
  only to find they did not yield the satisfaction we expected.
We have been let down by others
  and, worse still, we have let ourselves down
  on more occasions than we care to remember.
So often, hope ends in disappointment,
  exposed as wistful naiveté, misguided ambition or sheer foolishness.
Teach us, before all else, to trust in you,
  confident that your love will never fail or disappoint us.
Teach us to base our lives on your living word that promises so much
  yet delivers even more than we can ever ask or imagine.
In Christ's name.
Amen.

Intercession

General intercessions

283

Light of the world,
   shine wherever there is darkness today.
Where there is pain and sorrow,
   may the brilliance of your love bring joy.
Where there is sickness and suffering,
   may your healing touch bring sunshine after the storm.
Where there is greed and corruption,
   may your radiance scatter the shadows.
Where there is hatred and bitterness,
   may your brightness dispel the clouds.
Lord Jesus Christ,
   light of the world,
   rise again upon us we pray,
   and illuminate the darkness of this world
   through your life-giving grace.
In your name we ask it.
Amen.

284

Sovereign God,
   you turned the darkest of nights into the brightest of days
   through the resurrection of your Son,
   our Saviour, Jesus Christ.
Come now into the darkness of our world:
   into the night-time of suffering and sickness,
   doubt and despair;
   into the shadows of hurt and heartbreak,
   injustice and evil;
   into the bleakness of violence and hatred,
   fear and death.
May your new day dawn
   and the light of Christ blaze to your glory
   as we share his resurrection life,
   and rejoice in the victory he has won.
In his name we pray.
Amen.

285

Gracious God,
   we bring to you our broken world,
   racked by injustice and exploitation,

suffering and sorrow,
hatred and division –
so few signs of hope,
so much that invites despair.
We pray for those who work for change;
all who strive to bring help and healing,
hope and wholeness.
We pray for those who have stopped believing things can change:
all who have lost faith in themselves,
in others,
in life
or in you.
Gracious God,
bring healing and renewal;
finish your new creation among us.
May your will be done and your kingdom come,
through Jesus Christ our Lord.
Amen.

For the hungry and needy

286

Gracious God,
we have enough and more than enough,
but we know there are many deprived of even the basic necessities of life:
who go hungry while we eat our fill;
who have nothing to drink or wear,
no place to call their home,
no access to medicine or hospital care
and no opportunity to improve their lot.
Teach us not only to pray for them
but to respond to their plight by giving generously from our plenty,
in Christ's name.
Amen.

287

Gracious God,
we long for the day when your world will be as you want it to be:
a world in which you will lift up the lowly
and fill the hungry with good things;
in which love and justice shall triumph,
evil be ended
and the meek inherit the earth.
Give us confidence that such a day will come,
and, more than that, give us the resolve to help make it happen.

Help us to respond as best we can
    to the many millions who cry out for help,
    and so to play our part in bringing the dawn of your kingdom closer
    and turning vision into reality.
In Christ's name we ask it.
Amen.

288
Loving God,
    we are reminded today that, in terms of this world's resources,
    we are the lucky ones –
    those with food in our belly
    and a roof over our head,
    with ample water and medicine,
    and with access to education, technology and so much else –
    our lives brimming over with good things.
Forgive us our complacency in the face of the world's evils
    and our share in an order that not only perpetuates the divide
    between rich and poor
    but actively widens the gap.
Hear now our prayer for the millions less fortunate than us –
    those for whom hunger is a daily reality
    and for whom a lifetime of poverty is all that the future seems to offer.
Teach us to give sacrificially in response to their need
    and, more than that, to work for change,
    doing all in our power to help build a fairer world
    until that day when your kingdom dawns
    and all wrongs are righted.
We ask it in the name of Christ.
Amen.

289
Gracious God,
    we read in Scripture of good news for the poor
    and liberty for the oppressed,
    yet sometimes the reality appears very different.
Day after day,
    we hear stories of poverty, sickness, sorrow and suffering –
    some from far afield,
    some on our own doorstep.
All around us there seems to be so much injustice and oppression,
    hatred and evil.
We try to trust in your purpose,
    but the reality of this world seems to belie your will
    and contradict the gospel.

Reach out, we pray, wherever there is need,
    and grant that the light of your love may shine in our hearts
    and in the hearts of all,
    to the glory of your name.
Amen.

290
Loving God,
    hear our prayer for the have-nots of this world:
    those who have no homes,
    living as refugees or rough on our streets;
    those who have no food,
    their crops having failed,
    their economies burdened by debt,
    or their labours not fairly rewarded;
    those who have no fresh water,
    daily facing the threat of disease and the nightmare of drought;
    those who have insufficient resources to help themselves,
    condemned to a life of poverty with no prospect of respite;
    those who have no access to education, a health service
    or welfare system;
    no one to turn to for help or support.
Loving God,
    stir the hearts of all to work for a fairer world
    and a more just society.
Challenge all who have plenty to respond to those who have little,
    so that all may share in the riches of your creation
    and be able to celebrate your gift of life.
In Christ's name we ask it.
Amen.

For the lonely and unloved

291
Loving God,
    we pray for all who are lonely:
    those whose relationships have been broken
    or who have never enjoyed the relationships they might have had;
    those who feel rejected by society and unsure of their worth;
    those who spend day after day alone
    and those who feel hopelessly isolated even when they are in company.
Give to each one the knowledge that you are with them always,
    and enrich their lives with companionship and friendship.
In the name of Christ we ask it.
Amen.

For the sick and suffering

292
Loving God,
   we bring before you the sick and suffering of our world.
We pray for those afflicted in body:
   racked by physical pain,
   wrestling with disease,
   enduring painful surgery,
   or coming to terms with terminal illness.
We pray for those disturbed or troubled in mind:
   those whose confidence has been crushed,
   those no longer able to cope with the pressures of daily life,
   those oppressed by false terrors of the imagination,
   and those facing the dark despair of depression.
We pray for those afflicted in spirit:
   all who feel their lives to be empty,
   or whose beliefs are threatened,
   or who have lost their faith,
   or who have become caught up in superstition, black magic or the occult.
Living God,
   reach out through all who work to bring wholeness and healing.
Support and strengthen them in their work.
Grant them wisdom and guidance,
   strength and support,
   and the ability to minister something of your care and compassion for all.
In the name of Christ we ask it.
Amen.

293
Lord Jesus Christ,
   you spoke,
   and you brought hope, comfort and renewal;
   you touched,
   and you brought love, peace, healing and wholeness.
Come now,
   and speak again,
   bringing your word of life to all who suffer or are hurting.
Reach out afresh,
   bringing your touch of love to all whose hearts are aching
   and who cry out for help.
Where there is despair and turmoil,
   may your voice renew.
Where there is pain and sickness,
   may your hand restore.

Lord Jesus Christ,
   you came once,
   you shall come again,
   but we ask you,
   come now,
   and minister your grace,
   for your name's sake.
Amen.

For the sorrowful

see also Hope and despair; New beginnings: Resurrection hope

294

Loving God,
   we remember today all who mourn,
   their hearts broken by tragedy,
   tears a constant companion,
   laughter and happiness seeming a distant memory.
Reach out into their pain,
   heartache and sadness,
   and give them the knowledge that you understand their pain
   and share their sorrow.
May your arms enfold them,
   your love bring comfort,
   and your light scatter the shadows,
   so that they may know joy once more
   and celebrate life in all its fullness.
Amen.

295

God of all comfort,
   we bring you this world of so much pain:
   our own and that of those around us.
We bring you our hurts, troubles, anxieties and fears,
   placing them into your hands,
   and we pray for those countless others facing sorrow or suffering:
   hopes dashed,
   dreams broken,
   let down by those they counted dear;
   betrayed,
   abused,
   wrestling with depression or illness,
   mourning loved ones.
Hold on to us and to all who walk through the valley of tears.
Reach out and grant the knowledge that you are with us, even there,
   sharing our pain and moved by our sorrow.

Minister the consolation that you alone can offer,
   and give the assurance that those who mourn will be comforted
   and those who weep will laugh.
Lord,
   in your mercy,
   hear our prayer,
   in Christ's name.
Amen.

For those burdened by difficulties

296
Loving God,
   we pray for all who are bearing heavy burdens –
   those facing difficulties and problems to which they can see no solutions,
   wrestling with inner fears and phobias,
   racked by anxiety for themselves or loved ones,
   troubled about money, health, work or relationships –
   all who crave rest for their souls but cannot find it.
We pray for them and for ourselves,
   acknowledging that sometimes we too feel crushed under a weight of care.
Speak to all in your still small voice,
   and grant the peace and quiet confidence that only you can bring;
   and so may burdens be lifted and souls refreshed.
Lord,
   in your mercy,
   hear our prayer,
   in the name of Christ.
Amen.

For those who work for justice

297
Loving God,
   hear our prayers for all who seek to further your will here on earth:
   those who work for peace,
   who campaign for justice,
   who strive to relieve poverty,
   who fight for the hungry –
   all who struggle for the oppressed, the exploited,
   the under-privileged and those denied their proper rights.
Prosper their efforts
   and grant them inspiration
   so that they may challenge people everywhere to give of themselves
   in the service of others.

God of justice and mercy,
    hear our prayer,
    through Jesus Christ our Lord.
Amen.

298
Lord of all
    we pray for those who serve within the judicial system –
    barristers,
    lawyers,
    judges,
    magistrates,
    jurors
    and court officials –
    all those whose responsibility it is
    to see that justice is administered fairly to all.
Give them wisdom,
    integrity,
    courage
    and dedication,
    so that they may discharge their duties faithfully.
We pray for the police
    and all involved in the prevention or detection of crime,
    and we pray too for those who work in our prisons,
    in young offenders' institutions,
    in the probation or community services
    and in rehabilitation schemes.
Grant them help,
    guidance,
    strength
    and protection.
Lord of all,
    hear our prayer,
    through Jesus Christ our Lord.
Amen.

For those whose faith is faltering

299
Living God,
    we pray for those who find faith hard,
    those who want to believe but cannot get past their doubts.
We pray for those whose faith is wavering,
    undermined by the pressures and temptations of life.
We pray for those who have lost their faith,
    the fire that once burned within them extinguished.

We pray for ourselves,
    conscious that for us too faith can sometimes lose its spark.
For all those whose faith is faltering we pray:
    'Lord, we do believe,
    help us overcome our unbelief.'
Amen.

For victims of war

300
Lord of all,
    hear us now as we pray for victims of war.
We pray for those across the world who bear the scars of conflict –
    the injured, maimed and mentally distressed,
    those who have lost their limbs, their reason or their loved ones,
    their lives blighted by horrors of war.
We pray for those left homeless or as refugees,
    those who have lost their livelihoods and security,
    and those who still live in daily fear for their lives.
We pray for children who have been orphaned,
    for parents who mourn their children,
    and for husbands and wives who have lost their partners –
    countless families whose lives will never be the same again.
Lord of all,
    grant that the time will come
    when divisions will be overcome,
    evil conquered
    and hatred ended;
    a day when people everywhere
    will live in harmony
    and enjoy lasting peace.
Inspire all to work towards that goal,
    in the name of Christ.
Amen.

For those charged with decisions concerning war and peace

301
Living God,
    we pray for all whose decisions influence the stability of this world:
    for international leaders and rulers,
    for politicians and diplomats,
    for national governments and the United Nations council –
    those whose decisions and negotiations affect the lives of so many
    and in whose hands peace ultimately lies.

Grant them wisdom in all they do,
    courage to make tough decisions when necessary
    but also a desire to work for justice and peace whenever possible.
We pray for those in the armed forces,
    charged with keeping the peace in countries across the world –
    their work involving months away from family and friends
    and often danger to themselves.
Grant them courage and sensitivity,
    and protect them in all they do.
We pray for security and intelligence services
    in this world of so much uncertainty –
    those who work to forestall and prevent terrorism;
    to track down those who aim to destroy human life
    randomly and indiscriminately;
    to ensure the safety of all.
Grant them insight,
    determination,
    and skill.
Sovereign God,
    guide those entrusted with the future of this planet,
    so that the causes of conflict may be overcome
    and a more secure future ensured for all.
In the name of Christ we ask it.
Amen.

Kingdom of God

302
Gracious God,
   we mistakenly think sometimes of your kingdom
   in terms of the distant future –
   a time and a place yet to come –
   but you make it plain in the teaching of Jesus
   that it is already present
   and that you want each of us to commit ourselves
   to helping it grow here on earth.
Inspire us through all those who have had sufficient faith and dedication
   to attempt to do just that,
   catching a vision of what life can be,
   and striving to translate that vision into reality.
Help us to learn from them
   and to understand that you are at work in this world.
Teach us faithfully to offer our service
   and to work so far as we can to see your will done
   and your kingdom come in all its glory.
We ask it through Jesus Christ our Lord.
Amen.

303
Lord Jesus Christ,
   we talk so often about the coming of your kingdom
   that we can forget it has begun already,
   present among us in a host of ways.
In numerous expressions of love and kindness you are here,
   working out your purpose,
   serving and being served.
In countless lives being changed every day,
   you are here,
   calling,
   cleansing,
   renewing,
   restoring.
In the prayers, work and worship of your people,
   you are here,
   bestowing and making known your love.
The fulfilment may be yet to come,
   but the kingdom is here among us,
   dawning a little more brightly day by day.

Help us to play our part in its growth,
    to do what we can to make it more real on earth,
    until that day when we dwell with you and all your people
    in your eternal kingdom,
    and yours is the power and glory for evermore.
Amen.

304
Gracious God,
    you have promised that in the fullness of time your kingdom will come;
    a kingdom in which there will be no more war or violence,
    no more hatred or injustice,
    no more sickness, suffering or sorrow,
    but in which all will dwell in peace.
It is a vision that gives us hope and inspiration,
    and we long for the day when,
    together with all your people,
    we shall see it realised.
Yet there are times when it is hard to keep on trusting,
    a struggle to keep faith alive.
When we look at the sin and suffering in our world,
    the corruption, oppression and violence that seems so rife,
    we cannot help wondering if hope is simply a vain delusion,
    a chasing after the wind.
Teach us to go on believing,
    even when everything seems to count against such belief.
Help us to trust that your will shall be done,
    and, in faith, to do whatever we can,
    however small it may seem,
    to bring your kingdom nearer.
In the name of Christ we ask it.
Amen.

305
Loving God,
    sometimes we fail to see what is right there before us
    if only we would look harder.
Forgive us that this is so often true when it comes to your kingdom.
We look forward to the time when Christ shall return
    and we repeat the words of the prayer he taught us,
    'Your kingdom come',
    but we forget that he also proclaimed your kingdom is already here.
Loving God,
    teach us what that means.

Help us to understand that though the kingdom has been initiated through him,
  it must continue through us:
  through the service we offer
  and the life we live in his name.
Save us from being so concerned with what *will* be
  that we lose touch with what *is*.
In his name we ask it.
Amen.

306
Sovereign God,
  despite all that conspires against your purpose,
  you are at work in our world and at work in our lives.
You came in Christ,
  making yourself known,
  demonstrating your faithfulness,
  revealing the awesome nature of your love,
  and, through his ministry, you sowed the seeds of your kingdom.
You have worked since through countless generations of believers
  and you are working still,
  stirring hearts,
  quickening consciences,
  transforming lives,
  your light reaching out where there is darkness,
  your love offering new beginnings
  where the future had seemed hopeless.
Help us to glimpse your kingdom,
  to work for its fulfilment
  and to look forward in faith to that day
  when Christ shall come in glory
  to take up his throne and rule over all,
  to the glory of your name.
Amen.

Love

God's love for us

307

Gracious God,
   for all our talk of love we rarely actually show it.
We profess devotion, so long as nothing too much is asked of us.
We show affection, provided affection is returned.
Almost always, our love is conditional,
   as much about us as its intended object,
   dependent on *our* criteria,
   tied to *our* expectations.
Your love is so very different,
   constantly flowing out despite our unworthiness,
   despite everything about us that is unlovable.
You carry on reaching out though we reject you.
You continue to care for us though we care nothing for you.
Your love is qualified by no conditions,
   being entirely about us rather than you,
   our welfare,
   our joy.
Gracious God,
   you don't just talk about love –
   you show it day after day,
   for quite simply you *are* love!
To you be praise and glory,
   now and for ever.
Amen.

308

Lord Jesus Christ,
   before we ever loved you, you loved us;
   before we ever looked for you, you were seeking us out;
   before we ever made a response, you were guiding our footsteps.
Always you have been there taking the initiative,
   just as you did throughout your ministry
   and even at the time of your death.
In love you offered your life,
   and in love you continue to reach out,
   never resting until our journey is over
   and the race is won.
To you be praise and glory,
   honour and thanksgiving,
   now and for evermore.
Amen.

309

Gracious God,

   it is wonderful enough that you bother to look for us at all;

   more wonderful still that you keep on looking day after day,

   year after year,

   until you have found us.

No matter what we do or how often we fail,

   still we matter to you,

   enough for you never to rest until we are restored to your side.

Teach us to recognise the astonishing breadth of your love,

   and to respond with gratitude

   in faithful service

   and joyful praise,

   to your glory.

Amen.

310

Gracious God,

   we do not find it easy to love ourselves,

   despite the way it may seem.

We find it hard not to dwell on our weaknesses rather than our strengths,

   not to brood about mistakes and failures

   rather than rejoice in the things we have achieved.

We look at ourselves

   and we see the faults and ugliness that we try to hide from the world,

   and we find the reality too painful to contemplate,

   so we try to push it away once more.

Gracious God,

   we thank you that you love us despite all this,

   that you value us not for what we might become

   but for what we are.

Teach us to live each day in the light of the incredible yet wonderful truth

   that you love us completely

   and want us to be at one with ourselves,

   through Jesus Christ our Lord.

Amen.

311

Gracious God,

   we praise you that, above all else, you are a God of love –

   not of judgement, anger or vengeance,

   but of constant and total love.

Though we repeatedly fail you,

   turning our back on your goodness,

   still you continue to love us,

   fiercely and wholeheartedly.

Though we turn away from you,
    wilfully rejecting your guidance
    and repeatedly betraying your trust,
    still you long to take us back,
    to restore a living, loving relationship with you.
For this awesome love,
    greater than words can express,
    deeper than we can begin to understand
    and more passionate than anything else we shall ever experience,
    we give you our thanks and offer our worship,
    in the name of Christ.
Amen.

312
Gracious God,
    we talk often about love,
    but we have little idea what it really is.
The love we show to others is invariably flawed,
    corrupted by ulterior motives and self-interest.
We can scarcely begin to fathom the immensity of the love you hold for us;
    a love that is inexhaustible,
    awesome in its intensity,
    devoted beyond measure.
Forgive us for losing sight of this one great reality at the heart of faith
    without which all else is as nothing.
Forgive us for portraying you as a God of vengeance and justice
    when, above all, you are a God of love,
    a God who, despite our repeated disobedience,
    refuses to let us go.
Teach us to open our hearts to all you so freely give us,
    and so may we love you and others
    with something of that same total commitment.
We ask it in the name of Christ.
Amen.

313
Lord God,
    so many words are used to describe you,
    in an attempt to sum up just who and what you are.
We speak of your power, might and majesty
    to express your greatness.
We label you eternal, everlasting, infinite
    to convey your timelessness.
We speak of your justice, righteousness and holiness
    to encapsulate your otherness.

We call you Creator, Father, Redeemer
  to articulate your goodness.
Yet all these words fall short,
  pointing to part but not all of the truth.
We praise you, though, that there is one word that says it all –
  that little word 'love'.
However overworked the term may be,
  it nonetheless sums up your whole nature, purpose and being.
So, then, may we live each day,
  assured that, whatever may be,
  your love will always enfold us until it finally conquers all.
Lord God,
  we praise you,
  through Jesus Christ our Lord.
Amen.

314
Lord Jesus Christ,
  like so many others we yield to pressures to conform
  in our yearning for acceptance.
We wear a socially acceptable mask,
  say the right words
  and do what's expected of us rather than risk rejection,
  even when it means pretending to be what we are not.
We are so used to acceptance being conditional
  that we find it hard not to approach you in the same way,
  feeling that we must measure up to some yardstick
  of what is pleasing to you.
Teach us that your love is not like that.
Help us to recognise that even when we fail you,
  your love is not withdrawn.
May the knowledge that you accept us as we are
  help us each day to become more fully the person we can be,
  through your saving grace.
Amen.

315
Lord Jesus Christ,
  we are reminded today that you didn't just *accept* death for our sake
  but *chose* it;
  that you didn't simply let things happen
  but planned them in advance,
  knowing the way you would take,
  down to that final agony on the cross.

You staked all,
   you gave all,
   and you did it willingly for the sake of people like us.
Such love is too wonderful to comprehend,
   but we thank you for it with all our hearts,
   and offer you our joyful praise in glad response.
Amen.

316
Lord Jesus Christ,
   you came to our world as light in its darkness.
You came out of love,
   bringing life, hope and forgiveness.
You came not to condemn but to save,
   not to judge but to show mercy.
You came willingly enduring darkness for our sakes:
   the darkness of loneliness and rejection,
   of betrayal and denial,
   of suffering and humiliation,
   of fear and death,
   of all our human sinfulness carried on your shoulders.
Lord Jesus Christ,
   we thank you,
   we praise you,
   and we worship you.
Amen.

Loving others

317
Lord Jesus Christ,
   you didn't just talk about love;
   time and time again you showed it.
And you didn't just love those who loved you,
   but your enemies equally,
   those who you knew were intent on destroying you
   by whatever means necessary.
We stand ashamed, in contrast,
   our own love so weak,
   so limited,
   so dependent on its object.
Even loving our friends is hard enough;
   to love our enemies is beyond us;
   and yet we know that only this can break the cycle
   of hatred, suspicion and fear,
   which so divides our world.

Lord Jesus,
  we cannot achieve it ourselves,
  but, we ask you, move within us,
  touch our hearts,
  and teach us to love,
  for your name's sake.
Amen.

318
Lord Jesus Christ,
  forgive us that so often we love only ourselves,
  our every thought for our own welfare,
  our own ends,
  our own esteem,
  our own pleasures.
Forgive us that, at best, we reserve our love for the exclusive few –
  family, friends and relations.
Teach us to reach out to this troubled, divided world,
  recognising the call of our neighbour in the cry of the needy.
Teach us what it means to belong not just to the community of faith
  but also to the family of humankind,
  and in serving them may we equally serve you,
  to the glory of your name.
Amen.

319
Lord,
  we are told that the strongest survive –
  that in this world it's a question of never mind the rest
  so long as we're all right.
Yet you call us to another way –
  to the way of humility, sacrifice and self-denial.
You stand accepted wisdom on its head,
  claiming that the meek shall inherit the earth
  and that those who are willing to lose their lives
  will truly find them.
Lord,
  it is hard to believe in this way of yours,
  and harder still to live by it,
  for it runs contrary to everything we know about human nature,
  yet we have seen for ourselves that the world's way
  leads so often to hurt, sorrow and division.
Give us, then, courage to live out the foolishness of the gospel,
  and so to bring closer the kingdom of Christ
  here on earth.
In his name we ask it.
Amen.

320
Lord Jesus Christ,
  you summed up the law in one simple word: 'love'.
Forgive us that though we often talk about love
  we rarely show it in practice.
Forgive us everything in our lives that has denied that love:
    the angry words and unkind comments,
    the thoughtless deeds and careless actions,
    the sorrow we have brought rather than joy,
    the hurt rather than healing,
    the care we have failed to express,
    support we have refused to offer,
    and forgiveness we have been unwilling to extend.
Help us to look to you who showed love in action –
    a love that bears all things,
    believes all things,
    hopes all things,
    endures all things –
    and help us truly to realise that unless we have that,
    then all our words, faith and religion count for nothing.
Amen.

321
Gracious God,
    we marvel that you can love people like us,
    for there is so little about us that deserves it.
We look into the mirror of our souls
    and we are ashamed of what we see there,
    for the image is marred by greed, pride, selfishness, envy
    and so much else that destroys not just others but ourselves too.
Yet, incredibly, you value us to the point that we are precious in your sight,
    special enough even to die for.
If *you* can accept us, despite everything,
    teach *us* to do the same
    and, in learning to love ourselves as you do,
    help us also to love others and love you,
    through Jesus Christ our Lord.
Amen.

_____ Maturity in Christ, growth in _____

see also Faith: Growing and continuing in faith

322

Living God,
   we know what our lives ought to be like,
   we know what they are,
   and we are ashamed at the difference between the two.
Where we ought to reveal Christ,
   we show only ourselves.
Where we ought to bear witness to his life-changing power,
   we demonstrate instead how little has actually changed.
So much about us denies rather than affirms the gospel,
   leading people to dismiss its claims
   rather than to explore them further.
Forgive us for all that is wrong
   and, by your Spirit, clothe us with joy,
   peace,
   patience,
   kindness,
   generosity,
   faithfulness,
   gentleness,
   self-control,
   and, above all, love.
Work in our lives,
   and so work through us to speak to others,
   through the grace of Christ.
Amen.

323

Living God,
   we talk of commitment,
   yet so often we are casual about our faith
   and complacent in discipleship.
We neglect your word
   and fail to make time for prayer or quiet reflection,
   thus giving ourselves little opportunity to hear you.
Instead of seeking to grow in faith,
   we assume we have advanced as far as we need to.
Forgive us our feeble vision and lack of dedication.
Instil in us a new sense of purpose and a greater resolve to fulfil our goals,
   and so help us to achieve the prize

to which you have called us in Jesus Christ,
for his name's sake.
Amen.

324
Almighty God,
through Christ you have demonstrated the wonder of your goodness,
the awesome extent of your love.
You call us to follow in his footsteps –
to reflect through our lives and witness
more of that same gracious love.
Forgive us for failing to do that –
for failing to show in our lives the faith we profess with our lips.
Forgive us that all too often the picture we give is a feeble caricature,
a pathetic parody of the Lord we so hunger to serve.
Take, then, what we are
and, by your grace, make us what we long to be,
so that we may truly bring glory to you,
through Jesus Christ our Lord.
Amen.

325
Living God,
forgive us for being content to drift along
with little sense of direction or purpose;
for assuming it is enough to get by,
and failing to ensure that we do even that.
Give us courage to examine ourselves honestly,
to take stock of our lives carefully and prayerfully,
to face up to truth and see ourselves as we are,
and glimpse what we could and should be with your help.
Help us to tackle the things we prefer to push aside,
pretending they are not there –
to recognise our weaknesses as well as our strengths,
our faults as well as our virtues.
So may we grow each day in faith
and live more fully to your praise and glory,
through Jesus Christ our Lord.
Amen.

326
Lord Jesus Christ,
there is so much within us that is not as it should be:
thoughts, attitudes, desires and fears
that alienate us from others and from you
and that disturb, divide and ultimately destroy.

We long to be like you:
    to feel the same love and compassion that you felt,
    to experience the same closeness with God,
    and to know the same inner wholeness and harmony.
Alone, though, we cannot achieve it,
    no amount of effort sufficient to help us emulate your example.
Draw closer to us through your grace,
    and fill us in body, mind and soul.
Speak to us,
    teach and guide,
    so that we may know you better.
Work within our hearts,
    transforming the clay of our lives into a new creation,
    moulded by your hands.
In your name we ask it.
Amen.

327

Lord Jesus Christ,
    we thank you that discipleship is not finally about what *we* can do for you
    but about what *you* have done for us.
We praise you that your love does not depend on our works
    but on your grace.
We celebrate with wonder your presence within us;
    the way you have come into our lives
    to offer your guidance, strength, peace and joy.
Fill us a little more each day,
    so that we may know you better and become more like you,
    our lives testifying to your sovereign and renewing power.
Amen.

328

Lord,
    there is so much in the gospel that goes against the grain:
    your call to deny ourselves and put others first;
    your command to love our enemies and turn the other cheek;
    your challenge to forgive and go on forgiving.
All this,
    and so much else,
    runs contrary to our natural inclinations,
    contradicting the received wisdom of this world.
We do not find it easy and at times we resist,
    yet we know that in you and you alone is the path to life –
    the way to peace, joy and fulfilment.

Take us, then, and fashion our lives according to your pattern,
 until your will becomes our will
 and your way our way.
In the name of Christ we ask it.
Amen.

329

Living God,
 we thank you for the seed of faith you have sown within us
 and for the way it has grown across the years,
 but we confess also that there are times when all is not as it should be.
Instead of continuing to flourish,
 our commitment starts to flag and our vision to wilt,
 cramped by the narrowness of our horizons,
 suffocated by complacency and starved of space in which to expand.
Forgive us for allowing that to happen and accepting it as the norm.
Help us to open our lives to you
 so that you can feed us through your word,
 nourish us through your Spirit
 and nurture us through the gracious love of Christ,
 in whose name we pray.
Amen.

330

Living God,
 we turned to you once
 and, naively, we imagined we had done all that needed doing;
 that from then on we would say goodbye to our old self
 and live in newness of life.
The reality, we have found, is that two selves war within us.
Help us, then, to turn to you once more,
 and to go on doing so for however long it takes.
Help us, each day, to put off the old self
 and to be renewed in body, mind and spirit through your grace,
 until in the fullness of time you have finished your redemptive work
 and made of us a new creation,
 through Jesus Christ our Lord.
Amen.

_____ New beginnings _____

see also Christian seasons: Easter

331

Lord Jesus Christ,
   just as you brought new out of old
   through your fulfilment of the Law and the prophets,
   so also continue to make us new,
   taking our old self and refashioning it by your grace
   into a new creation.
Help us to let go of everything in our past that denies and destroys,
   separating us from your love.
Take what we are and re-create us by your power,
   so that we may be the people you would have us be,
   for we ask it in your name.
Amen.

332

Lord Jesus Christ,
   we are not good at letting go of the past,
   at recognising there are times when we need to move on in life;
   to take a step forward in faith if we are ever truly to grow.
We prefer the security of the familiar,
   the comfort of that which does not stretch or challenge us too far,
   and we are wary of the prospect of change,
   afraid that it might ask more of us than we are willing to give.
We are not good at letting go of the old and putting on the new,
   at turning away from our former way of life
   and taking instead the way of the cross.
We are reluctant to abandon old habits,
   fearful of being thought different,
   unwilling to deny ourselves the pleasures of this world
   for the promise of the world to come.
So we try to keep a foot in both camps,
   to combine the old self with the new.
We think we can balance the two,
   but, of course, we can't,
   and the result is that we compromise both
   and embrace neither.
Help us to understand that, while the old has its place,
   there are some areas in life where a complete break is needed,
   a turning away from what has been,
   before we are ready to receive what shall be.

Lord Jesus Christ,
  you want to work within us to finish the new creation you have begun.
Give us courage to trust you completely,
  so that you may refashion our lives to your glory.
We ask it in your name.
Amen.

333
Loving God,
  we praise you for the way you have worked in our lives:
  the way you have offered us a new beginning,
  a new identity
  and a new sense of purpose,
  constantly working within us to refashion and redeem us.
We thank you that, despite our weakness,
  you are able to take and use us far beyond our expectations.
Forgive us everything within us that frustrates your will,
  and, by your grace, continue to draw us to yourself,
  remaking us as a living testimony to your sovereign saving love,
  through Jesus Christ our Lord.
Amen.

334
Loving God,
  we thank you for the gift of this and every day.
We praise you for all the possibilities each brings,
  the innumerable opportunities for love, joy,
  fascination and fulfilment that every one opens up.
Teach us to count our blessings
  and to welcome this day as your gift,
  consecrating it to your service in grateful praise,
  through Jesus Christ our Lord.
Amen.

335
Living God,
  we praise you for springtime,
  this season of hope and anticipation,
  of shoots bursting into life,
  of new growth and a fresh start.
For making all things new, we worship you.
We praise you for the springtime we celebrate each day as Christians:
  life bursting from the tomb,
  light breaking into the darkness,
  faith dispelling doubt
  and hope triumphing over despair.

For making all things new, we thank you.
We praise you for the springtime you make possible each moment,
   your gracious love constantly offering a new beginning,
   the slate wiped clean,
   the page turned over.
For making all things new, we adore you.
Living God,
   receive our praise,
   accept our worship,
   and continue your renewing work within us,
   through Jesus Christ our Lord.
Amen.

Resurrection hope
see also Christian Seasons: Easter; Hope

336
Living God,
   through Jesus Christ you have taught us to pray,
   'Your kingdom come,
   your will be done.'
We look forward to the day when that prayer is answered –
   a day when there shall be no more night,
   no more tears,
   an end to mourning and crying and pain,
   an end to death itself.
Sustain us, we pray,
   through all the uncertainties of our fleeting lives
   with that sure and certain hope,
   and help us to live each day in the knowledge
   that one day you will be all in all.
Amen.

337
Lord Jesus Christ,
   you came to bring us life in all its fullness;
   to offer hope beyond the grave.
Teach us that death is not the end,
   but a new beginning –
   the gateway to life everlasting.
And may that confidence shape our attitude not only towards death
   but towards life also.
May we live each day not just in the context of the here and now
   but of eternity,
   knowing there is nothing in heaven or earth
   that shall ever finally be able to separate us from your love.
Amen.

338

Loving God,
> despite our faith there are times when we find life difficult,
> when situations seem hopeless,
> when we look to the future
> fearfully wondering what good it can possibly hold.

Help us to understand that the truth of resurrection
> is not just limited to the future,
> to life after death,
> but is about the present,
> life now!

Help us to realise it speaks not just about eternal issues
> but about our daily lives –
> the ordinary, the commonplace and the mundane.

Help us to understand that even there,
> and especially there,
> you bring resurrection.

Amen.

339

Loving God,
> we praise you that in Jesus
> you experienced not just life but also death –
> that you endured the darkness of Gethsemane,
> the agony of the cross
> and the finality of the tomb,
> triumphing over everything that keeps us from you.

We thank you that where the world saw only defeat,
> you brought victory,
> nothing able to stand against your sovereign purpose.

May that knowledge bring hope
> to all for whom life is overshadowed by death;
> a new perspective bringing light
> into the pain and sorrow of such moments.

Grant the assurance that death is not the end but a new beginning,
> a stepping stone into your glorious kingdom
> in which death shall be no more
> and where all will rejoice in the wonder of your love,
> for evermore.

Amen.

340

Lord Jesus Christ,
> you promise new life to those who follow you –
> not just a different quality of life here and now,

though that is a part of it,
   but life beyond the grave,
   life eternal.
Thank you for the way you foreshadowed that promise
   during your earthly ministry,
   demonstrating your sovereign, life-giving power.
You raised Lazarus,
   you raised the daughter of Jairus,
   you raised the son of a widow,
   and finally, after three days in the tomb,
   you rose yourself!
Through word and deed,
   you have given us the assurance that nothing in life or in death
   can ever separate us from your love.
Lord Jesus Christ,
   the resurrection and the life,
   we praise you.
Amen.

341
Lord Jesus Christ,
   just when it looked all over,
   when the world had written you off
   and even your disciples had given you up,
   you came back –
   defeat revealed as victory.
Teach us what that means for us today:
   not only the promise of eternal life,
   but also good news for life here and now.
Help us to understand that whatever tragedies we may suffer,
   whatever obstacles we may face,
   whatever disappointments we may experience,
   we can bounce back from them with your help,
   for you are a God able to transform even the darkest moments
   and to lead us through them into the light of your love.
Gladly, then, we put our hand in yours,
   knowing that in life or death you will never fail or forsake us.
To you be praise and glory,
   now and always.
Amen.

Peace

Living as peacemakers
see also Relationships: Disagreements, dealing with

342
Loving God,
   we talk so glibly of peace
   but find it so hard to pursue it.
We speak of breaking down barriers and living in harmony,
   but when it comes to being peacemakers,
   we so often fall short.
Forgive the many things within us that make for conflict –
   our pride, greed, envy and intolerance,
   our nursing of petty grievances and unwillingness to forgive,
   our preoccupation with self and lack of time for others –
   so much that pulls apart rather than draws together.
Make us instruments of your peace.
Teach us to heal wounds rather than create them,
   to unite rather than divide,
   to reconcile rather than separate.
Put a new spirit within us –
   a spirit of love and openness,
   acceptance and understanding,
   healing and reconciliation.
May the peace we so often pray for
   begin here and now with us,
   in the name of Christ.
Amen.

343
Gracious God,
   we look at the world sometimes,
   and we despair.
We see its greed, corruption, hatred and violence,
   and we can't help asking,
   'How will it ever change?'
We want to believe,
   and occasionally our hopes are rekindled by moves towards peace,
   yet it is hard to keep faith when, time after time,
   such initiatives come to nothing.
Gracious God,
   help us to recognise that our way of looking at the world

is not the same as your way,
   and that where we see no prospect of change,
   you are able to transform situations beyond recognition.
Teach us never to lose sight of all that you are able to do
   and all that you are already doing.
Inspire us, therefore, to pray for
   and, in our own small way,
   work towards peace and reconciliation,
   through Jesus Christ our Lord.
Amen.

344
Lord of all,
   we long to see peace in our world,
   but the disturbing truth is that faith itself
   seems to contribute towards division.
We look at history,
   and across the centuries we see a sorry catalogue
   of atrocities in the name of religion.
We look at the Church,
   and even today, despite all the efforts to build unity,
   there is still suspicion between various factions,
   to the point sometimes of outright hostility.
We know this shouldn't be,
   and yet we know also that peace doesn't come easily,
   for it can never be achieved
   simply through covering over the causes of our division.
Help us, then, to work for peace in whatever ways we can,
   but give us the faith and the courage we need
   to accept the consequences that may result from our efforts,
   until one day, at last, your will is done,
   your kingdom comes
   and all things are made new,
   through Jesus Christ our Lord.
Amen.

Peace of mind
see Fufilment, true nature of

Power of God
transforming nature of

345
Living God,
  we imagine sometimes that our lives are in our own hands,
  ours to shape as we will.
We fondly believe ourselves able to meet the rough with the smooth,
  to withstand adversity and bounce back after disappointments.
On occasions it's true,
  but equally there are times when it's patently false,
  experience painfully teaching us how fragile is our hold on happiness
  and how limited our resources to face life's demands.
Teach us to remember that true power lies in you –
  not as the world understands it in any show of strength
  but in an unshakeable confidence,
  an inner peace
  and a living faith
  through which your Spirit is able to work and move
  beyond all expectations.
Open our hearts to that mighty and mysterious presence,
  and so may we discover power for living,
  in Jesus' name.
Amen.

346
Living God,
  we praise you for your sovereign power
  through which you have transformed our lives,
  bringing strength, joy, hope and peace.
We thank you for the power that flows within us through Christ
  and the living presence of the Holy Spirit,
  equipping us to see life in a new way
  and to meet each day with confidence.
Yet we are conscious that you want your life-changing power
  to flow through us,
  reaching out into the world beyond.
Forgive us that we have failed to let that happen,
  so concerned with self
  that we have forgotten our responsibility to others.
Forgive the narrowness of our vision that has led us to store up,
  rather than be conduits of,
  your renewing grace.

Move within us,
   and open our lives to all that you are able to do,
   so that in your name we may live and work for you,
   through Jesus Christ our Lord.
Amen.

347
Loving God,
   for all our protestations of faith
   there are some things we consider to be not only beyond us
   but beyond you as well.
Hope says one thing but realism another,
   and in consequence we set limits
   on the way you are able to work in our lives.
Forgive us for doubting your power
   and questioning your ability to work in our lives.
Remind us of the way you have overturned human expectations
   throughout history,
   demonstrating that all things are possible for those who love you.
Teach us, then, to look beyond the obvious and immediate,
   and to live in the light of your sovereign grace,
   which is able to do far more than we can ever ask or imagine;
   through Christ our Lord.
Amen.

348
Loving God,
   there are times when you call us to tasks that seem beyond us,
   responsibilities we would rather avoid.
We hear your voice but we do not feel up to the challenge,
   our natural inclination being to run away.
Yet if you ask anyone to do something
   you always give the strength to do it.
Give us courage, then, to respond when you call,
   knowing that however things may seem,
   you are always able to transform them
   in ways far beyond our expectations.
Amen.

349
Loving God,
   we did not choose you –
   you chose us.
You are the one who opens the way for us to know you,
   who breaks down the barriers that keep us apart,
   who holds the future in your hands.

Help us to remember that
    and to be open to all the possibilities it presents.
Save us from presumptuously limiting you to our own narrow expectations,
    or from thinking that we can map out our destiny.
Teach us that you are a God of the unexpected,
    a God always waiting with new surprises to enrich our lives.
Amen.

350

Sovereign God,
    the challenges you set before us may be very modest
    compared to those others have faced over the years,
    but they can seem daunting nonetheless.
We feel inadequate to meet the task –
    acutely conscious of our lack of faith,
    the limitations of our gifts
    and our inability to serve you as faithfully as we would wish.
Yet, throughout history,
    you have repeatedly taken the most unpromising of material
    and used it in ways defying all expectations.
You have turned doubt into faith,
    weakness into strength,
    and timid service into fearless discipleship,
    and you go on doing that today through the power of your Holy Spirit.
Give us, then, the faith we need to respond to your call,
    trusting that, whatever you ask of us,
    you will be by our side to help us see it through,
    to the glory of your name.
Amen.

351

Sovereign God,
    we remember how you have changed the lives of so many across the years,
    turning fear into courage,
    uncertainty into confidence,
    denial into affirmation.
Remind us that as you changed them,
    so you can also change us;
    that you are constantly at work
    nurturing our faith,
    strengthening our commitment
    and deepening our experience of your love.
Open our hearts to the movement of your Spirit,
    so that we may give you freedom to mould and shape us to your will,
    and so make us the people you would have us be,
    to your praise and glory.
Amen.

_____ Praise and thanksgiving _____

see also Greatness and wonder of God

352

Eternal and sovereign God,
   with awe and wonder we worship you.
You are all-powerful,
   ever present:
   shaping the pattern of history,
   transforming our lives.
You are all good,
   ever merciful:
   showering us with your blessings,
   forgiving our faults.
You are always true,
   ever constant:
   daily fulfilling your purpose with the same dependability.
You are all holy,
   ever perfect:
   just and righteous in all you do.
Forgive us that we have not worshipped you as fully as we should;
   that we have not praised you with heart and soul and mind;
   that we have glimpsed so little of your greatness.
Forgive us for failing to appreciate your mercy,
   for forgetting your countless blessings,
   and for losing our sense of awe and wonder before you.
Open our eyes afresh to your splendour,
   our hearts to your love,
   our minds to your purpose
   and our spirits to your presence,
   and so may we thrill to the wonder of all that you are,
   in the name of the living Christ.
Amen.

353

Living God,
   we know that you do not need our praise,
   but we want to give it to you nonetheless,
   for you have blessed us in so much.
We want to acknowledge your goodness
   and thank you for the constancy of your love.
We want to show our appreciation for the wonder of life
   and tell you how much it all means to us.

We want to express our gratitude for your unfailing grace,
    the forgiveness you so freely and faithfully offer.
Living God,
    we do not simply *want* to say these things;
    we *need* to,
    for our hearts burns within us in joyful celebration.
So we come to you again now
    in grateful adoration
    and heartfelt worship.
Hear our prayer
    and receive our praise,
    in the name of Christ.
Amen.

354
Lord,
    we have so much to thank you for,
    yet all too often we take it for granted.
Instead of counting our blessings,
    we dwell on our frustrations.
Instead of celebrating everything you have given,
    we brood about the things we don't have.
In pursuit of illusory dreams of happiness,
    we lose sight of the gifts that each day brings,
    the countless reasons we have now to rejoice.
Forgive us for forgetting how fortunate we are,
    and help us to appreciate the wonder
    of all we have received from your loving hands.
Amen.

355
Sovereign God,
    higher than our highest thoughts,
    yet always close by our side;
    greater than we can ever imagine,
    yet made known to us in Christ;
    more powerful than words can express,
    yet having a special concern for every one of us –
    we worship you.
We praise you that, though we wander far from you,
    always you seek us out;
    though you sometimes seem distant,
    always you are near;
    though life seems to make no sense,
    still you are present,
    your purpose unchanging,

your hand reaching out to bless.
Sovereign God,
   we give you thanks for the assurance that brings,
   the hope for this life and the life to come.
Hear our prayer,
   in the name of Christ.
Amen.

356
Sovereign God,
   you are the giver of life,
   the root of all our being,
   the Creator of the ends of the earth,
   of all that is, and shall be, and has been.
Loving God,
   you give purpose to our lives,
   a sense of meaning to every day,
   a mood of hope as we look to the future,
   an inner confidence whatever we may face,
   and so we praise you.
Living God,
   you are with us always,
   imparting strength,
   giving guidance,
   offering comfort,
   and so we adore you.
Saving God,
   you have come to us in Christ,
   revealing your goodness,
   demonstrating your love,
   expressing your care,
   and so we honour you.
Gracious God,
   you are the giver of more than we can ever deserve,
   granting your constant blessing,
   surrounding us with your unfailing love,
   providing for our deepest needs,
   and so we thank you.
Almighty God
   receive our praise,
   our thanks,
   our worship,
   for we bring it to you in grateful response to all your goodness,
   through Jesus Christ our Lord.
Amen.

Joyful response

357

Gracious God,
 you give to us out of love,
 pouring out ever more blessings day after day.
Forgive us for sometimes giving to you out of habit or duty.
We bring an offering in worship because it is expected.
We make time for personal devotion because we feel we ought to.
We respond to others only when our conscience pricks.
The results may seem worthy enough,
 but the true value is small.
Teach us instead to give joyfully,
 not because we must but because we may.
Teach us to offer our money, our worship and our service
 as a gesture of love and an expression of our gratitude.
Help us to understand that it is not the gift that matters
 so much as the spirit in which it is given,
 and may that awareness inspire us to offer ourselves freely to you,
 in Christ's name.
Amen.

358

Great and wonderful God,
 you have blessed us in so much,
 showering us with your love and blessings.
Your goodness is greater than we can ever hope to measure,
 your love beyond anything we can even begin to fathom,
 your gifts more than we can start to number,
 and yet we know you as a living reality in our hearts,
 as the one who gives shape and purpose to all of life.
So we come to you with grateful hearts in joyful homage,
 seeking, as best we can, to make our response.
We consecrate this time to pray,
 to read,
 to think
 and to learn.
We acknowledge you as our Creator,
 our Lord,
 our Father
 and our friend,
 and we thank you for your incredible and unfailing love.
Accept now our worship,
 poor though it is and inadequate though our words may be,
 for we bring it to you as an expression of our gratitude

and a sign of our commitment,
    through Jesus Christ our Lord.
Amen.

359
Mighty God,
    enthroned in splendour,
    crowned with glory,
    ruler over all,
    we owe our life to you.
Eternal God,
    moving throughout history,
    giving your word,
    calling your people,
    we owe our hope to you.
Living God,
    full of love,
    full of kindness,
    full of compassion,
    we owe our joy to you.
Gentle God,
    speaking through your Spirit,
    through the quietness,
    through your still, small voice,
    we owe our peace to you.
Gracious God,
    abounding in love,
    slow to anger,
    rich in mercy,
    we owe our all to you.
Lord of all,
    our strength and shield,
    our rock and our fortress,
    our God and our Redeemer,
    we owe our worship to you.
Receive our praise,
    through Jesus Christ our Lord.
Amen.

360
Loving God,
    we bring you our worship not because we must but because we may,
    not because we have to but because we want to.
We come not out of duty but privilege,
    not because it is expected of us

but because you have graciously invited us to respond.
Receive our joyful worship and glad thanksgiving,
　　our love, our faith and our service,
　　for we offer them freely to you
　　just as you offered yourself freely for us,
　　through our Lord and Saviour,
　　Jesus Christ.
Amen.

361
Loving God,
　　we have so much to thank you for –
　　so much that is good and special.
Day after day you bless us,
　　week after week you answer our prayers,
　　year after year you meet our needs.
We cannot thank you enough for your great goodness,
　　yet the truth is that we rarely thank you at all.
Forgive us for taking your gifts for granted,
　　for letting familiarity blind us to how fortunate we are,
　　and so failing to thank you for all you have given.
Forgive us for being swift to ask for your blessing
　　yet slow to acknowledge your generous in giving it.
Teach us to receive your innumerable gifts with heartfelt gratitude,
　　and to show our thanks not just in words but also in our daily living –
　　in lives that gratefully celebrate the wonder of your love.
In Christ's name we ask it.
Amen.

362
Loving God,
　　we praise you that you do not just give us happiness, but also joy;
　　a sense of celebration that bubbles up within us,
　　irrepressible and indestructible.
We thank you that even when life is hard,
　　even when we are confronted by tragedy and disaster,
　　there is always a reason to rejoice,
　　springing from a confidence in your eternal purpose.
Help us to open our lives more fully to you each day,
　　so that our joy may be complete
　　and may communicate itself to others in such a way
　　that they too may come to celebrate your love
　　and exult in your blessing,
　　through Jesus Christ our Lord.
Amen.

363
Sovereign God,
   we thank you that you came in Christ
   not to exact punishment but to show mercy;
   not to restrict but to liberate;
   not to deny but to affirm.
Forgive us for sometimes turning joyful faith into sombre religion,
   the living gospel into lifeless dogma,
   a message of hope into a foretelling of doom.
Teach us to receive the gifts you want us to enjoy
   and to turn life into a celebration of your goodness.
So may the people we are,
   as well as the words we say,
   truly proclaim the good news of Jesus Christ.
In his name we ask it.
Amen.

364
Lord Jesus Christ,
   we can never repay all we owe you,
   nor even a fraction of what we have received
   from your loving hand.
There are no words or deeds great enough
   to thank you for all your goodness,
   but we yearn to make some kind of response,
   to express our gratitude for all you have done for us.
You have poured out your blessings,
   day after day,
   filling our lives with good things.
You have met our needs and more than our needs,
   showering us with untold riches.
Receive our worship,
   receive our faith,
   receive our love,
   for we bring them to you
   as a small but simple way of saying thank you.
Amen.

365
Great and wonderful God,
   we join with the great company of your people
   on earth and in heaven,
   to celebrate your majesty,
   to marvel at your love and to rejoice in your goodness.
You are our God,

and we praise you.
We acknowledge you as the Lord of heaven and earth,
   ruler of space and time,
   Creator of all,
   sovereign over life and death.
We salute you as the beginning and end of all things,
   the one who is greater than we can ever begin to imagine,
   higher than our highest thoughts,
   beyond human expression.
We affirm you as all good,
   all loving and all gracious.
We bring you now our worship,
   our faith and our lives,
   offering them to you in grateful adoration.
You are our God,
   and we praise you,
   through Jesus Christ our Lord.
Amen.

Songs of praise service

366
Lord,
   we thank you for the gift of song;
   for its ability to move, challenge and inspire us,
   its power to express feelings of joy and sorrow, hope and despair,
   its capacity to sum up our feelings in grateful hymns of praise.
Teach us when we worship to use this gift thoughtfully,
   singing to you from the heart,
   and offering not just the song but ourselves with it.
Teach us to reflect on the words we sing,
   so that they may speak *to* us of all that you have done
   and speak *for* us of all we would do for you.
O Lord,
   open our lips,
   and our mouth shall declare your praise.
Amen.

Prayer

see also Call of God: Voice of God

Asking in faith

367

Almighty God,
   yours is the purpose that brought the world and universe into being,
   and yet we try sometimes to impose our will on yours.
You are the Lord of heaven and earth,
   yet we imagine sometimes that we know best.
Yours is the hand that has led your people across the ages,
   yet we assume sometimes that our wish is your command.
Forgive us for reversing the roles and setting ourselves up in your place,
   seeking *our* ends rather than *your* will.
Teach us not just to speak of faith but also to live by it,
   trusting in your way,
   listening to your voice and working for your kingdom,
   through Jesus Christ our Lord.
Amen.

368

Gracious God,
   we don't have to tell you how weak is our prayer life,
   for you know it already,
   or how weak is our faith,
   for you can see that clearly.
We are afraid to pin too many hopes on prayer,
   in case you do not grant our requests.
We are hesitant to ask, in case we are seeking the wrong things.
Teach us that you are a God who listens and delights to respond.
Save us from the lack of trust that frustrates your purpose,
   preventing us from recognising your hand at work.
Give us ears to hear,
   eyes to see,
   and hearts that truly believe,
   through Jesus Christ our Lord.
Amen.

369

Lord Jesus Christ,
   we know that God hears our prayers,
   that he is ready to answer when we call to him,
   but we are still reluctant sometimes to ask for help,
   for we are conscious of having asked so many times before.

We seek forgiveness for the same old mistakes.
We ask for answers to the same old problems.
We look for guidance concerning the same old matters.
We intercede for the same old people.
Day after day,
    week after week,
    we bring the same list of requests,
    so familiar that even *we* have grown tired of them,
    let alone him.
We are afraid of exhausting his patience,
    of becoming an irritation and a nuisance,
    and we wonder whether we are asking for the wrong things,
    or whether perhaps God has given his answer,
    only we have failed to hear.
Yet you tell us he is always ready to listen,
    always wanting to bless,
    and that no matter how often we approach him
    he will make time to hear us and time to answer.
Teach us, then, to approach with confidence
    and to bring all our needs in faith before him,
    assured that he longs to meet our need
    and that, in the fullness of time,
    he will respond.
In your name we ask it.
Amen.

370
Loving God,
    you long to shower us with blessings,
    to fill our lives with good things,
    yet there are times when, through our weakness of faith,
    we frustrate your gracious purpose
    and deprive ourselves of the inexpressible riches you so freely offer.
We do not seek,
    so we do not find.
We do not ask,
    so we do not receive.
We concern ourselves with the fleeting pleasures of the moment
    and so fail to grasp treasures that endure for eternity.
Forgive us the shallowness of our values
    and the limitations of our understanding.
Teach us to set our hearts on those things that can truly satisfy,
    and that you so yearn to share with us.
In the name of Christ we ask it.
Amen.

Essentials of prayer

371
Living God,
   forgive us our superficial understanding of prayer –
   the way we abuse and distort it,
   using it as a lever to coerce you
   rather than seeing it as a personal encounter
   through which we might grow closer to you each day.
Teach us to seek what you will,
   rather than what we desire;
   to be open to your guidance,
   however much it may conflict with our own wishes.
Teach us to obey your voice.
Amen.

372
Living God,
   you invite us to talk *with* you in prayer
   but instead we talk *at* you.
You invite us to seek your will
   but we attempt rather to impose our own.
You tell us that you know all our needs,
   yet we present you with a list of demands and requests.
Forgive us the way we misunderstand and abuse prayer.
Teach us not only to speak but also to listen,
   not just to seek but also to find,
   not simply to bring our requests but also to respond to your call.
Remind us that there is a time for words
   and a time to keep silent,
   and help us to make room for both.
We ask it in Christ's name.
Amen.

373
Loving God,
   we are good at talking about prayer
   but poor when it comes to praying.
We find that the words just don't come
   or we find ourselves repeating the same old things.
We speak of a conversation,
   but the reality is more typically a monologue,
   and on the rare occasions that we make time to listen,
   we struggle to hear your voice.
As a result we all too often give up,
   prayer pushed to one side,

conveniently forgotten,
until some tragedy or crisis awakens us to our need of you.
Forgive us for abusing prayer,
using it as an excuse to avoid real service.
Forgive us our misguided prayers,
looking only to our ends rather than yours.
Forgive us our neglect of prayer,
our reluctance to take it seriously or to devote time to you.
Teach us what it means to wrestle in prayer
and what it means to act in faith,
and so may we use your gift as you intended,
to the glory of your name.
Amen.

374
Living God,
there are times when we pray but the words just won't come,
and times when we simply don't know what to pray for.
There are times, too, when we forget to pray,
or when our prayers are casual and half-hearted,
squeezed in as an afterthought at the end of the day.
We thank you, then, that we are not alone in prayer,
and that your response does not depend solely on our own efforts.
We thank you for the work of the Spirit within,
articulating our deepest thoughts and needs,
and we praise you for the faithfulness of Christ,
constantly interceding on our behalf.
Living God,
hear *our* words now
and *their* prayer always,
and, in your mercy, reach out in love.
Amen.

375
Gracious God,
we thank you that we can open our hearts to you,
that we can pour out our innermost souls
and share our deepest thoughts
in the knowledge that you are there,
always ready to listen and understand.
So once more we lay our lives before you,
open to your gaze:
the bad as well as the good,
the doubt as well as the faith,
the sorrow as well as the joy,
the despair as well as the hope.

We bring our feelings of anger as well as peace,
   of hatred as well as love,
   of confusion as well as certainty,
   of fear as well as trust.
We bring them honestly to you,
   so that we may discover the renewing love that only you can offer –
   a love that frees us to live as you would have us live,
   and that allows us to be the people you would have us be!
Hear now our prayer,
   in the name of Christ.
Amen.

When prayer seems unanswered
see also Questions of faith

376
Living God,
   there are times in our lives,
   all too many,
   when our prayers don't seem to be answered.
There are times when, for all our striving,
   we do not hear your voice or understand your will.
Yet you *do* respond,
   if only we have ears to hear and eyes to see –
   through the people around us,
   through the events of life,
   through the voice of conscience.
In a whole variety of ways you prompt us,
   not dictating our every step,
   not mapping out the future,
   but inviting us to share in the work of your kingdom
   and the fulfilment of your purpose.
Living God,
   help us to listen –
   help us to hear.
Amen.

377
Lord Jesus Christ,
   it is hard to keep faith when you do not seem to answer our prayers;
   harder still when you seem remote and disinterested,
   seemingly unmoved by our pleas.
Teach us that sometimes
   you are speaking precisely through that apparent lack of response,
   challenging us to look more deeply into our situation
   and to broaden our horizons.

Yet teach us also that you do hear and delight to respond,
    and so may we never be discouraged from asking,
    in your name.
Amen.

378
Living God,
    we bring to you those times when we call to you for help
    and you seem to be silent;
    those days when we do not hear your voice
    no matter how we listen for it.
Help us to understand that even when we feel alone,
    you are listening,
    and even when you seem far away,
    you are always near.
Give us faith to hold on,
    courage to trust in your promises,
    and humility to recognise that your answer will come
    in your own time and your own way.
May that knowledge sustain and inspire us,
    whatever we may face,
    through Jesus Christ our Lord.
Amen.

Questions of faith

see also Faith; Prayer: When prayer seems unanswered

379
Eternal God,
  there are times when we find life a puzzle,
  your purpose a mystery,
  experience seeming to contradict everything we believe about you.
We try to make sense of it all,
  but without success,
  satisfactory answers always seeming to elude us.
Teach us at such moments to trust in you,
  recognising that what the world counts as folly
  is often true wisdom.
Help us to live with riddles and apparent paradox,
  and to keep on searching for truth,
  confident that in the fullness of time
  you will make all things clear.
We ask it in the name of Christ.
Amen.

380
Gracious God,
  we thank you for all you have revealed to us in Christ
  and for the faith you have put into our hearts,
  but we thank you also that there is more to understand
  in our continuing journey of discovery.
So we bring you the things we don't understand,
  the statements of faith that don't seem to make sense
  and the events of life that seem to contradict
  what we have been taught of you.
We bring you our certainty and our uncertainty,
  those areas where faith is sure
  and those where it teeters on the edge of collapse.
Give us sufficient trust to acknowledge our questions openly
  and to offer them honestly to you in prayer.
Save us from taking refuge in ritual or dogma,
  but teach us rather to face the challenges that life brings
  and to work through our faith in the light of them,
  so that, having been tested, it may grow the stronger,
  able to face all and still to stand,
  through Jesus Christ our Lord.
Amen.

381

Living God,
  day by day we have to choose,
  to make decisions about right and wrong,
  good and evil.
Sometimes the choice is clear, sometimes confusing,
  sometimes easy, sometimes hard,
  sometimes mattering little, sometimes much,
  but, whatever the case, we need to seek your will
  and to make up our minds as to the best way forward.
Help us to decide wisely,
  for there is so much we do not understand,
  so many complicated and confusing areas of life.
Grant us faith to wrestle with such matters,
  confident that you can use them to lead us to new insights
  and a deeper awareness of your sovereign purpose,
  to the glory of your name.
Amen.

382

Living God,
  there is so much suffering in this world of ours,
  so much pain, sorrow and evil.
It is hard sometimes to reconcile all this with it being your world too,
  created by you and precious in your sight.
We search desperately for answers,
  clinging first to this and then to that,
  and underneath there are times when our faith begins to crumble.
Teach us that, though we cannot always see it,
  you are there,
  sharing in our anguish,
  carrying in yourself the agony of creation
  as it groans under the weight of imperfection.
Teach us that you will not rest until that day when all suffering is ended,
  when evil is no more
  and your kingdom is established,
  and in that assurance give us strength to face each day,
  whatever it might bring.
Amen.

383

Lord,
  you know our faith isn't perfect.
There is much that we don't understand,
  much that we question,
  and much that is not all it ought to be.

Despite our love for you,
   we find it difficult to trust as we know we should,
   the things we don't believe triumphing over the things we do.
Yet, for all its weakness,
   you know that our faith is real,
   and you know that we long to serve you better.
Take, then, what we are and what we offer,
   and, through your grace, provide what we lack
   until the faith we profess with our lips may be echoed in our lives,
   and our faith be made complete.
Amen.

384
Loving God,
   sometimes we cannot help but ask 'Why?'
'Why me?'
'Why this?'
'Why anything?'
There is so much we do not understand,
   so much that apparently contradicts our faith,
   leaving us groping for answers,
   and all too easily we feel guilty about having such questions,
   afraid that somehow we are letting the side down through doing so.
Yet in our hearts we know there is no point pretending,
   for we can never deceive you.
So help us rather honestly to admit that
   there are things we cannot make sense of,
   and to trust that though *we* may never understand,
   you do.
Amen.

385
Loving God,
   we *do* believe.
We believe that in Jesus
   you have shown the way, the truth and the life.
Yet alongside faith there is also doubt.
We do not have all the answers,
   and sometimes we seem only to have questions.
Yet we believe that those questions, honestly asked,
   can lead us to a deeper understanding of who you are
   and what you have done.
So today we offer you not just our faith
   but also our doubt,
   praying that you will use both to lead us closer to you.
Amen.

386
Sovereign God,
  we cannot help wondering sometimes about the justice of life.
We see so much that is wrong,
    so much that we cannot make sense of,
    and we ask ourselves why you stand by and let it happen.
Day after day, we watch helplessly as truth is trodden underfoot,
    love exploited,
    and the innocent suffer,
    while those who least deserve it seem to flourish.
Help us, confronted by such enigmas,
    not to lose heart.
Teach us to recognise that loving you brings its own rewards,
    greater than any this world can offer,
    and remind us also that the time will come
    when everyone will answer to you,
    and justice will prevail.
Amen.

387
Mighty God,
    there are times when life doesn't seem fair,
    when those who openly flout your will seem to prosper
    while those who follow you gain scant reward.
We know this shouldn't matter –
    that our treasure should be in heaven rather than on earth,
    our hearts set on things eternal rather than the riches of this world –
    yet it's hard sometimes not to feel frustrated,
    even resentful,
    at the apparent injustice of life.
Forgive us the times we have made that mistake,
    setting ourselves up as judge and jury.
Forgive us the times we have doubted you in consequence,
    questioning your justice and resenting your grace.
Teach us to understand that, whoever we are,
    our actions will finally catch up with us,
    and so help us to live faithfully as your people,
    rejoicing in the blessings you have given,
    and anticipating the joy yet to come.
Amen.

388
Eternal God,
    we find it hard sometimes to keep on believing
    faced by the cold realities of this world.

Life brings us joy and beauty,
    but it brings also pain and sorrow,
    times occasionally so testing that they stretch faith to the limit.
Tragedy and disaster strike us all,
    irrespective of virtue,
    untold suffering afflicting the most innocent.
We cannot make sense of it,
    try though we might,
    and we cannot help wondering sometimes why you allow it.
Yet you have shown us through your suffering and death in Jesus
    that you are not remote from our need,
    but a victim of it,
    sharing in our grief,
    enduring our sorrow,
    feeling our pain.
You faced and triumphed over everything that denies your love,
    giving us the promise that one day such things will be over.
We can't pretend this answers all our questions,
    but it reminds us that your heart bleeds for us
    and longs to tend our wounds.
Teach us to hold on to that insight,
    until that day when your kingdom comes,
    through Jesus Christ our Lord.
Amen.

389

Lord Jesus Christ,
    we thank you that you are the one who makes sense of faith –
    the one who enables us to grasp something of the mystery of God
    and to reconcile this with the riddle of life
    and the complexities of the world.
We thank you that you are the key that unlocks the door,
    opening up for us the way to understanding
    and to life in all its fullness.
Save us from getting bogged down in what we cannot understand,
    from barring the door to your love by restricting faith
    to our own limited understanding.
Help us always to look to you,
    and, through receiving your grace,
    may we follow your way
    until that day when we pass through the gates of your kingdom
    into the glory of God –
    Father, Son and Holy Spirit.
Amen.

390
Lord,
   so often we don't understand what is happening to us.
We are swept along by a tide of circumstances
   and we look in vain to find any pattern
   that might give meaning to it all.
Our fleeting span is a confusing riddle
   from which you can seem painfully absent.
Yet you are there, even though we cannot see you,
   patiently weaving the broken strands of life into an intricate tapestry.
Teach us, then, to trust in you and to live by faith
   until that day when the picture is complete
   and we understand at last all the ways you have been working
   to bring order out of chaos,
   good out of evil,
   joy out of sorrow,
   and life out of death.
In Christ's name we pray.
Amen.

391
Loving God,
   we do not want to be tossed around by every wind of change
   or swayed by every passing idea,
   but neither do we want to be so set in our ways
   that we are closed to new insights into truth
   and fresh perspectives on your word.
Forgive us those times when we have been just that,
   so convinced of our own rightness
   that we have refused to hear what others are saying –
   closing our ears to that which unsettles us
   and shying away from the possibility
   that our horizons need to be broader.
Give us true humility to listen to other opinions,
   to explore different possibilities,
   to face searching questions,
   and to adapt our views where appropriate,
   confident that truth is strong enough to be tested
   and to emerge the stronger for it.
In the name of Christ we ask it.
Amen.

392
Sovereign God,
   stronger than we can ever comprehend,
   greater that we can ever imagine,

wiser then we can ever understand
and more loving than we can ever dream,
teach us to consecrate our minds to you,
as well as our hearts,
using our intellect to wrestle with questions of faith
and to grow in understanding.
Yet teach us also when we need to recognise
the limitations of the human mind.
Show us when we need simply to trust,
knowing that you are a God above all gods,
made known through Christ our Lord.
Amen.

Relationships

see also Confession and forgiveness: Forgiving others

Anger

393

Living God,
   teach us when it is right to be angry:
   to rage against the things in life that demean and destroy,
   that feed injustice and further exploitation,
   that cheat, corrupt, wound and hurt,
   that lead the innocent astray
   and divide people from one another and from you.
Yet teach us also when anger is foolish and petty,
   more about our hurt pride than right and wrong,
   about ourselves than the cause we attribute anger to.
Save us, then, from the errors it might lead us into –
   thoughtless words,
   careless deeds,
   and destructive attitudes –
   and help us to control such anger before it controls us.
Amen.

394

Lord,
   we are not good at showing anger;
   at least, not as it is meant to be shown.
We are ready enough to show our temper,
   easily riled by the most innocuous of things,
   and capable, at our worst, of destructive fits of rage,
   but such anger is rarely justified,
   almost always serving merely to give vent to our feelings
   at the cost of someone else's.
Your anger is so very different,
   being not about yourself but us.
You see injustice and exploitation,
   and your blood boils for the oppressed.
You see the peddling of drugs and pornography,
   and your hearts burns within you at the innocent led astray.
You see hatred, violence and cruelty,
   and your spirit seethes for those caught up in its wake.
Whatever destroys hope,
   denies love
   or despoils life
   arouses wrath within you.

Teach us to share that anger and to channel it in your service,
  committing ourselves to do all in our power to fight against evil,
  and to work for the growth of your kingdom,
  through Jesus Christ our Lord.
Amen.

Disagreements, dealing with
see also Peace: Living as peacemakers

395
Gracious God,
  forgive us the foolish divisions we allow to come between us,
  the petty disputes that grow out of all proportion
  until they destroy even the most precious relationships.
We know there will always be occasions when we disagree,
  for we are all different,
  each having our own way of looking at the world
  and our own unique experience of life,
  but in Christ we should be able to see such diversity as a blessing
  rather than a threat,
  a source of strength instead of a cause of weakness.
Forgive us the pride and insecurity that prevents this,
  leading us instead to nurse anger, bitterness and resentment in our hearts.
Teach us to admit our mistakes whenever we are in the wrong,
  and when the fault lies with others,
  teach us to forgive freely as you have forgiven us.
Grant us the mind of Christ
  so that we may live in harmony,
  for his name's sake.
Amen.

396
Lord,
  it's easy to start a quarrel,
  so much harder to end it.
It's easy to see faults in others,
  far more difficult to see our own.
It's easy to destroy relationships,
  almost impossible to build them again once they have been broken.
Forgive us the weaknesses that so often create divisions,
  that separate us not simply from our fellow human beings
  but sometimes even from our own family and friends.
Help us –
  so far as it lies with us –
  to live in harmony with all,
  and when that harmony is broken

teach us to act as peacemakers,
　healing hurts, restoring trust and breaking down barriers.
We ask it in the name of Christ,
　whose love will finally bring reconciliation to all.
Amen.

Encouraging, enabling and respecting all

397
Gracious God,
　you call us to support one another,
　to offer comfort in times of need,
　reassurance in times of fear,
　inspiration in times of challenge,
　and confidence in times of doubt.
Forgive us for so easily doing the opposite –
　finding fault,
　running down,
　criticising and condemning.
Forgive us for seeing the worst instead of the best,
　for believing the bad instead of the good,
　for so often pulling down and so rarely building up.
Teach us to recognise people's gifts and nurture them,
　to understand their problems and share them,
　to acknowledge their successes and applaud them,
　to appreciate their efforts and affirm them.
Teach us, through the faith we show in people,
　to help them attempt great things and expect great things;
　to look at life seeing not the obstacles but the opportunities,
　not the things they can't do but the things they can.
So may we help them in Christ to discover their gifts,
　recognise their true worth and fulfil their potential,
　through his grace.
Amen.

398
Gracious God,
　we marvel today at the wonder and extent of your love;
　the fact that you came in Christ not simply to a few but to all:
　good and bad,
　lovely and unlovely,
　deserving and undeserving.
You reached out and accepted us as we are,
　with all our doubts and fears,
　faults and weaknesses.

You look deep into the hearts of all,
     and where we see ugliness,
     you see someone infinitely precious,
     so valuable that you were willing to endure death on a cross
     to draw them to yourself.
Forgive us that we find it so hard to accept others in turn,
     seeing the worst rather than the best,
     putting down rather than building up.
Break through our narrow judgemental attitudes
     and help us to see the special in people as well as the ordinary,
     loving others as you love us.
Amen.

399
Living God,
     sometimes we feel weighed down
     by the stresses and strains of daily life –
     oppressed by worry,
     unable to throw off our anxieties,
     held captive by a multitude of secret fears.
We thank you for all those who help us through such moments,
     who offer a shoulder to lean on,
     an arm to steady and a hand to share the load.
Teach us in turn to bear the burdens of others,
     doing all we can through listening,
     understanding,
     caring and sharing,
     to offer them our help.
As you have reached out to us,
     so teach us to reach out in turn,
     expressing your love and showing your care,
     to the glory of your name.
Amen.

400
Lord,
     we are so wrapped up in ourselves
     that we forget sometimes all we owe to others:
     the support, love, encouragement and inspiration
     we receive from so many.
We are swift to complain when things are not done
     but slow to express gratitude when they are,
     good at criticising
     but poor in showing appreciation.
Help us to recognise everything others do for us
     and to make a point of acknowledging it.

Help us to play our part in turn,
    contributing to their lives with equal commitment and dedication.
In Christ's name we pray.
Amen.

401
Loving God,
    we thank you that you are a God we can depend on,
    always there in times of need,
    our truest friend.
We thank you for all those we count as friends –
    those who we know will stand by us
    even when life is difficult and our fortunes low –
    and we thank you for the fellowship we share in Christ
    with all your people.
Help us to show true friendship in our relationships with others:
    to offer support in times of crisis,
    encouragement in times of fear,
    comfort in times of sorrow
    and hope in times of despair.
Help us to know you as our constant companion,
    standing with us in all that we face,
    and as you have been faithful to us,
    so help us to be faithful to you,
    through Jesus Christ our Lord.
Amen.

402
Loving God,
    thank you for always being with us, whatever we may face,
    to strengthen, encourage, comfort and protect.
Thank you for those around us who we can count on
    to be there when we need them.
Teach us through their simple yet vital ministry –
    their willingness to share our troubles and bear our burdens –
    that there is nothing we need face alone.
Teach us to share that ministry in turn,
    ready to draw alongside those in any kind of need
    and to offer support and companionship.
Help us to understand that it is not so much what we say or do
    that matters at such times,
    but simply being there.
So may we give expression to your love
    and bring home your presence,
    to the glory of your name.
Amen.

403

Living God,
   forgive us that we find it so easy to see faults in others
   and so hard to see them in ourselves.
Forgive us that we are so often negative and so rarely positive.
Teach us to see strengths rather than weaknesses,
   to lift people up rather than put them down,
   to nurture confidence rather than crush spirits,
   to recognise the good rather than dwell on the bad.
Put within us the Spirit of Christ,
   so that we may follow his way of love and acceptance,
   mercy and understanding.
In his name we ask it.
Amen.

404

Living God,
   we have been guilty of devaluing both others and ourselves.
We have seen weaknesses and failed to consider strengths,
   we have dwelt on failures and ignored success,
   we have looked at the outside
   instead of searching deeper beneath the surface.
Forgive us for overlooking our own potential
   and closing our minds to that in those around us.
Forgive us for finding it so easy to put people down
   and so hard to build them up.
Teach us to recognise that everyone has a place in your purpose
   and a contribution to make to your kingdom,
   and so help us to be open to everything you are able to do.
All this we ask through Jesus Christ our Lord.
Amen.

405

Gracious God,
   you have told us that in Christ there is neither Jew nor Greek,
   slave nor free,
   male nor female.
You tell us that you value us for what we are,
   and in countless lives you show this to be true.
In a world of prejudice and discrimination,
   you have repeatedly called people from all walks of life,
   all strands of society,
   each having a unique place in your kingdom
   and a vital contribution to make towards it.

Teach us, then, to see beyond the artificial barriers we create:
    to be open to all,
    to respect all,
    and to work together for your kingdom
    in the unity of your Son, Jesus Christ our Lord.
Amen.

406
Living God,
    when we are confronted by ideas we do not understand
    our natural tendency is to lash out against them.
We resort to the language of insult.
We condemn rather than try to understand.
We ridicule rather than reflect.
And, because of that, so often we fail to recognise you are speaking to us,
    challenging our preconceptions
    and leading us on to new experiences of your love.
Living God,
    when we meet ideas different from our own,
    give us grace to see them for what they are,
    and to recognise that it may be us rather than them who need to change.
Amen.

407
Lord Jesus Christ,
    you did not come to judge or condemn the world,
    but to save it.
Where others saw the bad in people,
    you saw the good.
You recognised the value in everyone,
    and instilled in all a sense of worth.
Such was your willingness to welcome the unacceptable
    that many were scandalised by your behaviour.
Forgive us that we can be equally self-righteous,
    more concerned with judgement than mercy.
Forgive us for failing to see in ourselves the evil
    that we are so ready to see in others.
Teach us to look at the world with your eyes,
    and to deal graciously in all our relationships,
    just as you have dealt graciously with us.
Amen.

408
Sovereign God,
    there is so much in our lives that separates us from you and others –
    our selfishness, pride, greed and envy;
    our thoughtless actions,

foolish words and selfish nature;
   our narrowness of outlook and blinkered preconceptions –
   so much that runs contrary to your will and denies your love.
We thank you that, through Jesus,
   you have broken down the barriers that divide person from person
   and humanity from you.
Help us and all your people to live in such a way
   that we reflect this truth in all we are and do.
Stir the hearts of all,
   so that the day may come
   when the worth of everyone will be recognised,
   their rights observed,
   their dignity respected
   and their good pursued.
In Christ's name we ask it.
Amen.

409

Father God,
   reach out to all who are lonely,
   deprived of human companionship through age or infirmity,
   or separated from others –
   even when they are with them –
   through fear,
   shyness,
   mistrust or prejudice.
Reach out into our fragmented society,
   in which so much of the feeling of community has been lost,
   where ties that once bound families together have been broken,
   where so many live only for themselves.
Father,
   give to us and to all a sense of worth
   and an understanding of the humanity that binds us together,
   through Jesus Christ our Lord.
Amen.

410

Gracious God,
   we know that you value each one of us,
   not for what we might become but for what we are.
Forgive us that, all too often, we forget that truth,
   full of our own importance,
   preoccupied with self,
   harbouring vain illusions about who we are and what we can achieve.
We have not valued others as they deserve,
   allowing prejudices and preconceptions to colour our judgement
   and poison our attitudes.

We have looked down on those around us,
   failing to see the good in them,
   closed to the contribution they can make to our lives.
For all those times when we have valued ourselves too much
   and others too little,
   forgive us
   in the name of Christ.
Amen.

411
Living God,
   we are guilty sometimes of forgetting our humanity,
   minimising the gulf between us
   and setting ourselves up in your place.
Yet at other times we are guilty of the opposite mistake,
   devaluing our humanity and belittling that of others.
We see weakness rather than strength,
   failure rather than potential,
   and errors rather than achievements.
We write people off rather than recognise their true worth;
   we expect the worst rather than believe the best;
   we fail to appreciate all that you are able to do in people's lives,
   including our own.
Living God,
   we understand so little of what it means to be human.
Speak to us now
   and in glimpsing your greatness
   may we discern more clearly our own worth and the worth of all.
In Jesus' name we ask it.
Amen.

412
Lord Jesus Christ,
   you do not want us to think too much or too little
   either of ourselves or of others.
You want us to recognise that everyone is important to you –
   none more so,
   none less –
   each of us unique in your sight,
   valued for what we are.
Help us to keep a sensible balance in life,
   to have a due sense of our own worth and that of others.
Above all,
   give us a constant awareness of your greatness,
   before which we can only bow in wonder,
   acknowledging our weakness beside your strength,

and may that realisation give us a proper perspective on all.
In your name we ask it.
Amen.

413

Sovereign God,
   we have been guilty of the sin of pride,
   thinking of ourselves more highly than we should,
   boasting of our own achievements
   and looking down on those around us.
We have not listened to your voice or the voice of others,
   believing instead that we know best,
   and we have been guilty of pride in more subtle ways,
   hiding our frailties behind a mask of self-sufficiency,
   denying our weaknesses and refusing support when it has been offered.
Forgive us, and grant us true humility:
   a willingness to listen to your voice,
   to recognise our weaknesses
   and to acknowledge our need of others,
   through Jesus Christ our Lord.
Amen.

414

Gracious God,
   we don't mean to put ourselves before you;
   it just happens.
We talk of your glory,
   but it is our own that concerns us.
We speak of bringing honour to your name,
   yet we waste so much energy nursing or nurturing our ego instead.
Forgive us the pride that lurks deep within,
   claiming the praise that is rightfully yours.
Forgive us our failure to follow and learn from Christ.
Teach us, as he did, to humble ourselves under your mighty hand,
   so that in your own time you may lift us up.
Amen.

415

Loving God,
   we talk about all people having a place in your kingdom,
   but we do not always live as though we believe it.
We try not to pigeonhole people according to the colour of their skin,
   their religion,
   their age
   or their gender,
   yet we have innate preconceptions

about what is acceptable and unacceptable,
and we write off anyone who does not conform to our ideas.
We see differences as a threat rather than a gift,
the prejudices within us running deep,
poisoning our very soul.
Teach us to look at people with your eyes,
seeing the good and the bad,
the lovely and the unlovely,
the strengths and the weaknesses,
yet seeing above all our common humanity.
Open our hearts and mind to others,
and so, in turn, to you,
through Jesus Christ our Lord.
Amen.

416
Sovereign God,
time and again you have overturned human expectations,
using the most unlikely of people in yet more unlikely surroundings.
You have shown beyond doubt that no situation or person
is outside the scope of your purpose –
that you can use each one of them.
Teach us, then, to be open to everything you would do
through those around us,
and to recognise also all you can do through us,
working in ways we would never dare to contemplate
and can scarcely imagine.
Sovereign God,
you recognise the potential of everyone and everything –
help us to do the same.
Amen.

417
Living God,
it is hard sometimes to say no.
We do not want to let people down.
We like to appear on top of things,
capable of meeting every challenge,
and we are reluctant to admit our limitations.
We are afraid of being thought selfish
or unwilling to put ourselves out.
For a whole variety of reasons,
we find it easier to say yes even when we know we should decline.
Teach us that there are times when we owe it to ourselves,
our family or our friends to say no,
and times also when saying yes

will mean a job is not done properly, if at all.
Help us to do what we can,
    both in your service and in the service of others,
    but to recognise also what we can't do,
    and then grant us the courage we need to say no.
In Christ's name we pray.
Amen.

Envy

418
Living God,
    you have given us so much;
    forgive us that we still want more.
We have so many blessings to rejoice in;
    forgive us that instead we dwell on the pleasures we do not have.
Above all,
    forgive us for the way we allow envy to poison our attitudes
    and colour our judgement,
    insinuating itself into the way we think, feel,
    speak and act towards others.
Teach us to appreciate everything that is good in our lives,
    and to rejoice equally with others in the things that are good in theirs,
    and, most of all, teach us to celebrate the love you give freely to all,
    beyond measure,
    without reserve,
    now and for all eternity,
    through the grace of Christ.
Amen.

Judging others

419
Almighty God,
    we have set ourselves up in your place so often,
    presuming we have a right to judge others.
We know it is wrong,
    and we try to stop ourselves,
    yet we repeatedly fall into the same trap,
    pointing the accusing finger in condemnation.
We jump to conclusions that say more about ourselves than anyone;
    we see faults in others
    yet we are blind to our own innumerable failings.
Forgive us,
    and help us to change.

Teach us to see the best rather than the worst,
to look for good rather than evil,
to build up rather than destroy.
Teach us to forgive as you have forgiven us,
and to leave final judgement where it belongs –
with you.
Amen.

420

Gracious God,
we know how foolish it is to judge by the outside,
yet time and again we catch ourselves doing it.
Our mind says one thing,
but our heart tells us another.
Even when we think we are looking deeper,
our conditioning makes us look at the world in a set way,
deceived by superficial impressions,
failing to see the good in some and the evil in others.
Help us to see with your eyes,
to look beyond the obvious to the deeper realities of life,
and to recognise the true worth of all those around us.
Amen.

421

Living God,
forgive us for imagining sometimes
that we know all there is to know about people;
for presuming to judge their abilities and qualities
on the basis of what we understand about them.
Forgive us for questioning what you can do through them
because we fail to see their true potential.
Teach us that you are able to use anyone and everyone
in ways we have not even begun to consider.
Open our eyes, then, to what you are doing in those around us,
and help us to recognise what you may be saying to us through them.
In Christ's name we ask it.
Amen.

422

Lord Jesus Christ,
we thank you that you love us and accept us
not for what we can be but for what we are.
We thank you that although you see our many weaknesses,
still you have time for us,
seeing the best rather than the worst.

Lord Jesus Christ,
  forgive us that all too often we see only the surface,
  judging people according to instant impressions,
  and condemning those who do not fit in with our view of the world.
Help us to have time for others as you have time for us.
Amen.

423
Loving God,
  you tell us not to judge others,
  but we find it so hard not to.
You tell us that on those occasions when we do need to judge,
  we should do so rightly,
  but again we find that so difficult,
  for although we strive to be open-minded
  and objective in the decisions we make,
  we all too rarely succeed.
We are shaped by a multitude of influences that make us the people we are,
  and the way we look at the world is determined by each one,
  so that we find it almost impossible
  to see beyond our preconceived ideas.
Even when the truth is staring us in the face we can fail to spot it,
  so ingrained have these ideas become.
Break through the barriers that shut our minds fast,
  and help us to see things both as they really are
  and as you can help them become.
Loving God,
  fill us with the mind of Christ,
  to his glory.
Amen.

424
Sovereign God,
  like the Pharisees of old
  we too are often guilty of finding fault with others
  when in reality the problem lies in ourselves.
We are so busy looking for things to criticise
  that we fail to recognise our own many weaknesses.
Day by day, we are guilty of hypocrisy
  without even beginning to realise it.
Forgive us for the way we preach one rule for others
  whilst reserving another quite different for ourselves.
Forgive us for dwelling on the letter of the law
  whilst completely overlooking the spirit.

Teach us to recognise that your will is summed up
   in one simple commandment:
    to love,
    and so work within us
    that your love may characterise our every thought and action.
In the name of Christ we ask it.
Amen.

425

Lord Jesus Christ,
   you have told us not to judge lest we be judged.
Yet so often we cannot help ourselves.
We jump to conclusions,
   coloured by the prejudices of others,
   and closed to all opinions other than our own.
Give us wisdom to recognise that we do not have all the answers,
   openness to ideas and insights other than our own,
   and patience to trust that in the fullness of time
   you will make your way clear to us.
Amen.

426

Sovereign God,
   there is much in this world that is corrupt
   and so much in society that is unjust,
   but we are often afraid to speak out against it
   for fear of the consequences.
Even when wrongdoing affects us personally
   we are reluctant to protest in case the result proves costly.
We are cautious about throwing the first stone
   in case it turns out we have misunderstood the situation.
We do not want to risk hostility or damage to our credibility.
We are afraid that once we nail our colours to the mast
   there may be no going back.
Sovereign God,
   you do not want us to judge,
   but you *do* want us to stand up for what is right
   and to oppose what is evil.
Help us to recognise when those times are,
   and give us courage then to be true to our convictions,
   and true to you.
Amen.

Laughter

427
Loving God,
   we thank you for the things in life that make us laugh,
   the things that bring a smile to our faces.
We thank you for a sense of humour
   helping us to see the funny side of life,
   enabling us to share a joke even when it is on us.
We thank you for those with the special gift of bringing laughter to others,
   bringing a little light relief into the seriousness of our world.
We know that there is a time to weep and a time to laugh,
   a place for solemnity and a place for humour –
   help us to get the balance right in our lives.
Teach us to appreciate your gift of laughter,
   and to share it with those around us.
We ask it in the name of Christ.
Amen.

Sensitivity towards others

428
Lord,
   we thank you for the wonderful gift of words,
   the ability through language to communicate with others,
   to express our thoughts and feelings,
   to share information,
   to move, challenge and inspire,
   to offer ideas,
   to bring comfort.
Forgive us for the way we turn something so special
   into something so ugly,
   capable of causing such devastation.
Teach us to think more carefully about what we say
   and to speak always with the intention of helping
   rather than hurting.
Help us to use words wisely,
   in the name of Jesus Christ,
   the Word made flesh.
Amen.

429
Loving God,
   forgive us all the times we have failed to listen to others,
   too preoccupied with our own affairs
   to hear what they were saying to us.

Forgive us the hurt we have caused,
   the needs we have overlooked
   and the opportunities we have missed to offer help,
   all because we have not had ears to hear.
Teach us to be open to what people are saying
   and sensitive to their situations,
   and so may we be ready to respond in the right way,
   at the right place and at the right time,
   through Jesus Christ our Lord.
Amen.

430
Loving God,
   so often we act with little or no thought
   as to the potential repercussions,
   only to find later that the results of decisions taken,
   whether our own or those of others,
   are hard to bear.
We act unkindly and cause untold hurt.
We speak hastily,
   and sow a seed that grows beyond our control.
We ignore your will and then find life has turned sour.
Help us to act wisely,
   carefully considering the future in all our decisions.
Help us to put right past mistakes and to learn from them.
Help us to think of the consequences before we do something,
   rather than afterwards when it is too late to change them.
We ask it in the name of Christ.
Amen.

Within the Church

431
Lord Jesus Christ,
   you call us to be your Church.
Not just some of us, but all of us –
   from different traditions,
   with varying patterns of worship and contrasting doctrines,
   but sharing the same faith,
   serving the same Lord,
   worshipping the same God.
We cannot pretend there is nothing that divides us
   but we know there is much more that unites us,
   and we know your greatest wish,
   possibly your dying wish,

was that we should be one,
   witnessing to the wonder of your love
   through the love we have for one another.
Help us then to hear your word,
   to respond to your Spirit,
   to show your love
   and to become the people you would have us be,
   for your name's sake.
Amen.

432
Lord Jesus Christ,
   your body was broken for us.
You endured the agony of the cross to reconcile us to God,
   to break down the barriers that divide us,
   to make us one.
Forgive us that we have erected new barriers in place of old,
   barriers that divide us from one another,
   that separate church from church and Christian from Christian.
Help us to recognise that you died not just for some but all of us,
   and so help us to understand that whatever keeps us apart
   can never be more important than what binds us together.
In your name we ask it.
Amen.

433
Gracious God,
   for all our talk of love and fellowship,
   we are not very good at loving others,
   too easily allowing divisions and differences to sour our relationships.
For all our talk of being part of your family,
   we close our minds to so many brothers and sisters in Christ.
Forgive us,
   and open our minds to the unity of faith
   that we share with your people in every place.
Give us a concern for and openness to all.
Fill your Church with love,
   and so bind us together,
   to the glory of your name.
Amen.

434
Gracious God,
   we thank you for the great honour of belonging to Christ
   and being part of his Body.

Teach us what that means.
Help us to contribute to the life of your people,
   through offering our time, money, gifts and service.
Help us to make time for fellowship,
   so that we may know the strength
   that comes through sharing joys and sorrows,
   joining in prayer and worship,
   and learning through the experience of others.
Help us to appreciate the enrichment
   that comes through being an active member of your family,
   and so may we make that membership more real each day,
   through Jesus Christ our Lord.
Amen.

435
Lord Jesus Christ,
   there are some people we find it easy to relate to,
   others we find hard;
   some we are naturally drawn towards,
   others we shy away from;
   some we enjoy working with,
   others who constantly rub us up the wrong way.
Yet you have called us into a family in which all have their place,
   however different they may be.
Teach us to see such differences as strengths,
   and help us to be ready to learn from others.
Amen.

436
Lord,
   we talk of being part of your family,
   of sharing in a special bond that nothing can break,
   yet so often such claims are only fine-sounding words.
When circumstances change
   and people move on,
   we soon drift apart from them,
   scarcely sparing them a second thought.
Forgive us,
   and awaken us to the opportunities we have to express our concern,
   and in doing that may we show something of your loving care for all.
In Christ's name we ask it.
Amen.

437
Loving Father,
    we thank you for the richness of your family:
    for the bewildering assortment of gifts,
    characters and temperaments within it,
    the contrasting experiences of your love,
    and the different ways in which knowing and loving you is expressed.
Teach us to celebrate that diversity
    and to rejoice in the rich diversity you have given.
Help us to learn from others,
    and so may our faith grow and deepen
    as we continue along our individual pathways of faith
    and on our pilgrimage together,
    through Jesus Christ our Lord.
Amen.

438
Loving God,
    you have called us into the fellowship of the Church,
    to work alongside your people for the growth of your kingdom.
You have called us into a family through which we can find support,
    encouragement,
    strength
    and inspiration.
Forgive us the many times we have lost sight of that truth,
    neglecting our responsibilities towards others
    and overlooking the contribution they can make to our lives in turn.
Forgive us for going it alone
    rather than standing alongside our brothers and sisters in Christ.
Forgive us for allowing apathy, selfishness, mistrust or differences of opinion
    to obscure the unity we should share in the gospel.
Open our eyes to everything we can give and receive,
    and so may our faith be enriched
    and our service renewed,
    to the glory of your name.
Amen.

Serving others

see also Cost of discipleship: Sacrifice and self-denial;
Faith: Faith in action

439
Lord Jesus Christ,
 you came into our world as the King of kings and Lord of lords,
 but you came also as the servant of all.
You came deserving praise and worship,
 yet willingly accepting mockery, rejection and suffering
 for our sake.
You came to bring life in all its fullness,
 yet you offered your life to redeem the world.
Teach us to recognise the values of your kingdom
 that turn *human* values on their head.
Help us to understand that we discover self when we lose sight of it,
 that we serve you when we respond to others,
 that we are lifted high when we are brought low,
 and may that realisation shape the kind of people we are
 and the life we live,
 to the glory of your name.
Amen.

440
Lord Jesus Christ,
 your words concerning love for our neighbour sound so wonderful,
 until we stop to ask what they mean,
 and then, suddenly, the scale of the challenge
 and the likely cost of discipleship
 dawn on us,
 and we wonder how we can even begin to respond.
Teach us that, though we can't do everything,
 we *can* do something.
Teach us that a little offered by many can achieve much by your grace.
Fill us, then, with your love so that we may love in turn,
 to the glory of your name.
Amen.

441
Sovereign Lord,
 there are things we can do by *ourselves* and things only *you* can do;
 there are times when we have the resources within us
 to cope with a situation
 and times when we depend utterly on you for help.

Teach us to know the difference
and help us to remember that though our reserves may run dry,
yours never will.
Give us, then, an appreciation of our abilities,
but, above all, an appreciation of yours,
through Jesus Christ our Lord.
Amen.

442
Lord Jesus Christ,
we thank you for the difference you have made to us and to so many;
and for the difference you have made to the world,
working through countless individuals
and transforming innumerable situations across the centuries.
You call us, in turn, to make a difference –
to bring joy, hope, help and healing to those who are hurting,
to all who have lost their sense of purpose or faith in the future.
Forgive us for failing so often to honour that calling,
our discipleship making such a feeble impact on those around us.
Teach us to reach out in your name
and to share in your renewing work.
Teach us to be salt of the earth,
fit for use in your service,
to the glory of your name.
Amen.

_____ Stillness and quiet reflection _____

443
God of peace,
   quieten our hearts
   and help us to be still in your presence.
We find this so hard to do,
   for our lives are full of noise and confusion,
   a host of demands and responsibilities
   seeming to press in upon us from every side,
   consuming our time and sapping our energy.
We run here and there,
   doing this and that,
   always something else to think about,
   another pressing matter demanding our attention –
   and then suddenly,
   in the middle of it all,
   we stop and realise we have forgotten you,
   the one we depend on to give us strength and to calm our spirits.
God of peace,
   we offer you now this little space we have made
   in the frantic scramble of life.
Meet with us,
   so that we may return to our daily routine with a new perspective,
   an inner tranquillity,
   and a resolve to make time for you regularly
   so that we may use _all_ our time more effectively
   in the service of your kingdom,
   through Jesus Christ our Lord.
Amen.

444
Gracious God,
   we thank you for this opportunity to worship you,
   these few moments set aside to listen,
   to reflect,
   to respond.
Forgive us that such moments are all too few;
   that we allow our time with you to be crowded out
   by other demands on our time.
There is always something else that needs doing –
   another letter to write,
   another meal to prepare,
   another job to finish,

another meeting to attend –
and so it goes on,
one thing after another calling for our attention
and forcing you to the back of the queue,
Gracious God, there *is* much that needs to be done,
but help us to understand that there is nothing as important
as spending time in your presence,
for without your strength, your peace and your renewing touch
we lose our perspective on everything,
depriving ourselves of the resources we most need.
Help us, then, not simply to find *some* place for you,
but to give you *pride of place*,
for only then will we experience the fullness of life
you so long to give us,
through Jesus Christ our Lord.
Amen.

445
Lord Jesus Christ,
time and again throughout your ministry you made time to be still,
to draw away from the crowds
so that in the quietness you could reflect on your calling.
You needed those moments,
just as we need them in our turn.
So now we have made a space in our lives,
away from the daily demands,
away from the usual routine.
We are here, Lord, with time for you,
in stillness and in quietness to seek your will.
Use these moments
to refresh us,
to feed us,
to challenge and inspire us.
Fill them with your love
and so may we be filled to overflowing,
by your grace.
Amen.

446
Loving God,
we talk of peace but all too rarely find it,
for our minds are full of a multitude of concerns,
which pull us this way and that
until we feel bewildered and confused.
We hear your still small voice bidding us to let go and rest,
but always there is another call,

another demand on our attention pressing in upon us,
   and before we know it your word is drowned in the noisy bustle of life.
We cannot ignore the world or our responsibilities within it,
   and we would not want to,
   for there is so much you have given us that is good,
   but help us always to make time for you within it,
   so that even when chaos seems to reign,
   your quietness may fill our souls
   bringing an inner calm that nothing will ever be able to shake.
In Christ's name we pray.
Amen.

447

Sovereign God,
   we are here to worship you,
   having made a space in our lives to pause and reflect.
We come to listen to your word,
   and to ponder in the silence what you would say to us.
We come to hear your voice,
   and in the stillness to receive your guidance.
Open our eyes to your presence,
   our hearts to your love
   and our minds to your will.
Direct our thoughts,
   enlarge our understanding,
   and shape our lives,
   so that we may live and work for you,
   to the glory of your name.
Amen.

447

Gracious God,
   you have promised to all who love you
   a peace that passes understanding.
Forgive us that we have failed to make this our own.
We rush about,
   our minds preoccupied by our problems.
We brood over situations that we cannot hope to change,
   magnifying them out of all proportion.
We worry about what the future may hold
   instead of focusing on the present moment
   and living each day as it comes.
Teach us that you hold all things in your hands
   and that, even when our worries prove justified,
   you will give us strength to get through.

Whatever clouds may appear on the horizon
   and whatever storms life might throw against us,
   may our minds be at rest,
   our spirits at peace and our hearts untroubled,
   through Jesus Christ our Lord.
Amen.

448
Living God,
   in the rush and bustle of each day we all too often lose sight of you,
   our minds occupied by the responsibilities,
   demands and difficulties confronting us.
Instead of turning to you,
   we get sucked in ever deeper,
   getting these out of all perspective
   and denying ourselves the strength we need to meet them.
Teach us to find time for you,
   if only for a few moments,
   so that we may hear your voice and discern your will.
Teach us to step back and take stock,
   so that we may then step forward,
   renewed in faith,
   strengthened in spirit,
   and equipped for whatever you may ask.
In Jesus' name we ask it.
Amen.

449
Living God,
   too often we rush from one thing to the next,
   preoccupied with the demands and responsibilities of each day,
   and wondering where we might find the strength to see us through.
Yet instead of turning to you we struggle on as best as we can.
Teach us to create space in our lives for you,
   to make a few moments every day in which we can be quiet and still,
   and teach us to do that not as an afterthought but instinctively,
   recognising that when we give you your proper place,
   everything else will fit into place as well.
In Christ's name we ask it.
Amen.

450
Loving God,
   in all the stress and rush of life it is so easy to forget you
   and to lose our way.

In the press of each day,
     preoccupied with our problems, pursuits,
     plans and responsibilities
     we allow you to be crowded out.
We strive and fret over things that cannot satisfy,
     we brood over what is unimportant,
     frantically suppressing that sense of emptiness deep within.
Teach us to untangle ourselves from everything that enslaves us
     and to open our hearts afresh to you,
     so that we might find rest and nourishment for our souls
     and life in all its fullness,
     through Jesus Christ our Lord.
Amen.

451
Loving God,
     we live at such a hectic pace,
     our lives so busy and pressurised,
     with never a moment to spare.
Yet so often we forget the one thing we really need:
     time to pause and ponder,
     to take stock of our lives and reflect on your goodness
     so that we might understand what it is that you would say to us.
Draw near to us now in these few moments of quietness.
Teach us to be still and to know your presence,
     through Jesus Christ our Lord.
Amen.

Strength in weakness

see also Greatness and wonder of God

452
Gracious God,
   there are times in our lives when we feel up against it
   and when everything seems to conspire against us.
We look at the problems confronting us,
   and we feel small and helpless,
   powerless to do anything about them.
Yet you are a God who, time and again,
   has used those who seem insignificant in this world
   to achieve great things;
   a God who has overcome the strong through the weak
   and who is able to accomplish within us
   far more than we can ask or even imagine.
Help us, then, when we are faced by obstacles that seem insurmountable,
   to put our trust in you,
   knowing that you will give us the strength we need,
   when we need it.
Amen.

453
Loving God,
   we haven't much to give,
   and of what we do have we give you only a fraction.
To think that you can use this stretches credulity to the limit,
   and yet, across the years, you have taken
   what the world regards as insignificant
   and repeatedly used it to transform situations.
Teach us, then, to look not at the feebleness of our resources,
   nor the awesome scale of human need,
   but to recognise instead your sovereign power,
   and so, in faith,
   may we offer our money,
   our witness
   and our service
   to the glory of your name.
Amen.

454
Sovereign God,
   Creator and ruler of all,
   forgive us that we lose sight sometimes of your greatness,
   forgetting the incredible resources you put at our disposal.

We look at the difficulties we face
   and we feel overwhelmed,
   questioning our ability to get through.
We look at the needs of the world,
   and we feel there is nothing we can do,
   no way we can make a difference.
We look at your call to discipleship,
   your summons to make disciples of all nations,
   and we feel it is utterly beyond us,
   such a mission beyond all credibility.
We measure the challenge against *our* ability to respond to it
   rather than yours.
We think only in terms of our feebleness
   instead of your awesome strength.
Come to us afresh through your Holy Spirit,
   and fill us with your power –
   the power of faith, love, courage and mercy –
   and so use us to fulfil your will
   and to bring nearer your kingdom,
   through Jesus Christ our Lord.
Amen.

455
Lord,
   there are so many challenges in life,
   so many obstacles we feel unable to face.
Whether it is the everyday pressures of life
   or the unique responsibilities of Christian discipleship,
   we question sometimes whether we can cope,
   convinced that we lack the necessary qualities, courage or commitment
   to meet them successfully.
Yet you have promised that whatever you ask anyone to do,
   you will enable them to fulfil it,
   your Spirit always there to encourage and your hand to guide.
Inspire us, then, to respond in faith,
   confident that, in your strength, no task is too hard to take on,
   and no challenge so daunting that we cannot meet it.
In Christ's name we ask it.
Amen.

456
Sovereign God,
   we praise you for the strength you have shown across the centuries,
   working in circumstances that seemed hopeless
   and through people who seemed powerless to do anything.

We praise you that you are able to transform situations
    in a manner that defies human logic,
    giving strength to the weak
    and achieving great things that look impossible.
Teach us never to measure a situation by the way things seem
    and never to avoid a challenge because we feel unable to meet it.
Help us to look to you
    and to trust in your strength that is stronger than any earthly power,
    recognising that whatever you set out to accomplish,
    you will do,
    through Jesus Christ our Lord.
Amen.

457

Sovereign God,
    you came to our world in Christ and you lowered yourself,
    taking the form of a servant,
    enduring suffering and humiliation,
    even finally death on a cross.
Yet through that sacrifice you won the greatest of all victories,
    triumphing over evil,
    scattering darkness,
    defe ating death itself.
What appeared to be weakness was shown as strength,
    what seemed like disaster was revealed as triumph,
    what the world deemed failure proved to be glorious success.
Teach us to recognise that now, as then,
    you turn lives upside down,
    working in the most unexpected of ways
    through the most unexpected of people.
Teach us that you can work in our lives too,
    taking our frail faith and feeble commitment,
    and using our weakness to demonstrate your glory.
Take us and use us for your kingdom,
    through Jesus Christ,
    the Lord yet servant of all.
Amen.

458

Loving God,
    we find it hard sometimes to shoulder our responsibilities,
    preferring instead to share the burden with others,
    but there are times when we have to stand on our own two feet
    and accept the challenges life brings.

Help us, when those moments come,
to recognise that, however helpless we may feel,
and however weak we may think we are,
we can rely on you to see us through.
Teach us that we are never alone,
for you are always with us,
giving us the help we need to meet
whatever challenges may lie ahead.
So, trusting in your strength,
may we faithfully discharge the responsibilities you give us.
Amen.

459

Loving God,
we do not like living with weakness.
We want to feel strong,
in control of our destiny,
able to stand up against whatever life might throw at us,
and we resent anything which threatens that sense of security.
Yet, across the years,
you have repeatedly turned this world's expectations upside-down,
your values totally different from our own.
You humble the proud,
you bring down the mighty,
you reduce the powerful to nothing,
choosing instead to work through those
who seem insignificant and vulnerable.
Teach us, then, when we find our weaknesses hard to accept,
to recognise that you are able to use them
in ways beyond our imagining,
and to understand that in those very weaknesses
your strength is most perfectly seen.
In the name of Christ we ask it.
Amen.

Temptation

see also Lent

460
Living God,
   we know that much in our lives is not as it should be;
   that we have allowed thoughts and deeds to creep in
   that inexorably eat away at our faith,
   poisoning our attitudes,
   and subtly destroying our relationship with you.
Help us to recognise that though you are always ready to forgive,
   such things slowly prevent us from recognising our need for forgiveness.
Teach us that, though we cannot successfully combat
   our weaknesses by ourselves,
   with your help we can be awake to their presence
   and find strength to resist them in times of temptation.
Strengthen and equip us to meet whatever tests we face
   and to walk faithfully with you,
   come what may.
In Christ's name we pray.
Amen.

461
Lord Jesus Christ,
   you were tempted just as we are and yet you did not sin.
Forgive us that we find it so much harder to resist temptation,
   our spirit willing but the flesh weak.
Forgive us that all our resolve can be undermined in just a few seconds
   as temptation repeatedly catches us unawares.
Renew and refashion us in your image,
   so that when we are tempted to go astray –
   to indulge our desires,
   ignore your will
   and excuse what we know to be inexcusable –
   we will have the inner strength to say no.
Touch our hearts and put a right spirit within us,
   so that in times of trial we may stay true to your way,
   by your grace.
Amen.

462
Living God,
   teach us never to underestimate the forces
   that conspire against our faith,
   but also never to neglect or undervalue

the resources you put at our disposal
to stand firm against their onslaught.
Keep us awake to the power of temptation
and aware of the many pressures that can lead to inner conflict.
Teach us to put you at the centre of our lives,
meeting you in your word,
relating to you in prayer,
proclaiming you with our lips
and honouring you with our lives.
So may we be equipped for battle
and ready to defend ourselves against whatever we may face,
through Jesus Christ our Lord.
Amen.

463

Living God,
there are times when we deliberately disobey you,
but more often than not we inadvertently let you down,
failing both you and others.
Save us from punishing ourselves over innocent mistakes,
but grant us also wisdom and insight,
so that we may be awake to temptation,
alert to pitfalls
and sensitive to pressures that might lead us astray.
Direct our steps,
and so help us to walk in your way,
by your grace.
Amen.

464

Loving God,
you know what it is to be tempted,
for you took on human flesh,
making yourself frail and vulnerable,
just as we are.
You know what it is to lose everything,
for you gave your only Son for the life of the world.
For our sake, you became poor,
enduring humiliation,
and yet you stood firm,
refusing to be swayed or to contemplate compromise.
Teach us, in turn, to hold fast when temptation comes,
to seek your will rather than follow our own inclinations,
to work for your kingdom rather than pursue our gratification.

Show us the way you would have us take,
   and help us to walk it faithfully,
   now and always.
Amen.

465
Lord,
   we thank you for the privilege
   of being able to worship and witness to you freely
   and of being able to read your word and declare your name
   without fear of recrimination.
Save us, though, from ever imagining
   that our faith is safe from challenge.
Remind us that we are part of a world
   in which Christian values are constantly being undermined,
   where greed and selfishness are held up as virtues,
   and where wealth and success have all too often replaced you
   as the real object of humankind's devotion.
Every day the pressure is there to conform –
   to give a little ground –
   first here,
   then there,
   until little by little our convictions are diluted
   and the distinctiveness of our faith destroyed.
Teach us to be awake to the dangers we face,
   and give us strength to resist them by holding fast to you.
Amen.

Time

God's timing

466

Living God,
   even in our lifetime so much has changed,
   so many things that we considered permanent
   turning out to be passing shadows.
It is hard not to be unsettled by it all,
   and harder still not to question whether anything is permanent,
   even your love.
We find ourselves all at sea,
   tossed here and there by the waves,
   overwhelmed by a sense of helplessness
   in stemming the relentless flow of time,
   and we look around in desperation for something to support us,
   a lifeline to keep us afloat.
Teach us to look to you,
   the one unchanging reality in a world that is constantly moving on.
Teach us that you alone offer a hope that endures
   a purpose that defies the ravages of the years,
   and so may we keep our eyes fixed on you,
   come what may,
   assured that though all else may fade away,
   your love will remain the same,
   unchanged and unchangeable.
In Christ's name we ask it.
Amen.

467

Gracious God,
   we praise you that in the shifting sands of time
   your purpose remains sure;
   that though all else may change,
   your love will never alter.
For the assurance you give us of your love in Christ,
   and for making that new each day
   through the living presence of your Holy Spirit,
   receive our thanks.
Teach us to live every moment in the light of your goodness,
   and so to be at one with you and ourselves,
   through Jesus Christ our Lord.
Amen.

468
Eternal God,
  ruler over space and time,
  before all,
  in all,
  and beyond all,
  we worship and acknowledge you,
  recognising afresh that your ways are not our ways
  nor your thoughts our thoughts.
Forgive us for sometimes losing sight of that fact,
  presuming that we know better than you;
  even expecting you to do our bidding rather than us do yours.
Teach us that you are beyond our greatest imagining,
  higher than our loftiest dreams,
  and that you do things in your own way and time.
Teach us, then, to trust in your timing
  even when it conflicts with our own;
  to accept our part in your scheme of things,
  and to leave the rest to you,
  through Jesus Christ our Lord.
Amen.

Wise stewardship of time

469
Gracious God,
  this is the day that you have made and we praise you for it.
Forgive us for so often failing to do that,
  frittering away what we have now
  through our preoccupation with what once was
  or what yet might be.
Help us to recognise each day as your gift,
  to be received with gratitude and lived to the full.
Teach us to welcome every moment as a new beginning,
  putting the past behind us,
  and working towards the future you hold in store for us.
This is the day that you have made –
  in Christ's name we will rejoice and be glad in it.
Amen.

470
Lord,
  we know it's foolish,
  that impatience gets us nowhere,
  but we just can't seem to help it.

We try telling ourselves, 'What's the hurry?'
We do our best to slow down,
    to take it easy.
We remind ourselves of what really matters.
Yet, before we know it,
    we find ourselves fretting once more
    about a few moments wasted here,
    a little delay there.
Touch us by your grace
    and teach us to receive every moment as your gift,
    living each one for what it is.
Put a tranquil spirit,
    a quiet mind
    and a patient heart within us,
    and help us to learn that the more we worry about time,
    the less we will enjoy the time we have.
Amen.

471
Living God,
    we spend so much of our lives in ceaseless striving,
    pursuing first this,
    then that.
We labour,
    we fret,
    we fight,
    we struggle,
    all our thoughts so often focused on present gain
    and immediate satisfaction.
Yet all the goals that consume us bring but a moment's pleasure,
    each destined to fade away.
Teach us to set our hearts first on you,
    and to discover the fulfilment you long to give us
    in both this life and the next.
Help us to live not just in the context of the brief span
    you have given here on earth,
    but in the light of your eternal purpose in which,
    by your grace,
    you invite us all to share.
Amen.

472
Lord,
    you have given us a multitude of gifts and opportunities;
    forgive us that we sometimes fail to use them.
We don't think of ourselves as lazy,

but time and again we avoid tasks which we ought to tackle,
  at a cost ultimately to ourselves,
  to others
  and even to you.
So many possibilities are wasted
  and so much peace of mind is lost
  because we prefer to put off till tomorrow
  what we ought to do today.
Teach us to make the most of each moment,
  to use our talents to the full,
  and to tackle every task as it comes,
  for both our sake and yours.
Amen.

Trust

see also Faithfulness of God; Hope and despair; Kingdom of God;
Will and purpose of God

473
Gracious God,
we want to trust you,
but we find it hard to do so sometimes.
We see problems rather than opportunities.
We remember failure instead of success.
We are filled with doubt rather than faith.
Like your servant Gideon, long ago,
we crave a sign,
some assurance that you will see us safely through.
Forgive us for finding it so difficult to rely on you,
for so easily forgetting all you have done for us.
We do not deserve any proof,
yet in your mercy you repeatedly provide the sign we are looking for.
Teach us to trust you without reserve,
and grant that we may draw closer to you
until we need no further confirmation of your purpose
than the daily, living reality of your presence.
Amen.

474
Loving God,
we thank you that in the turmoil of life you are always with us –
your love reaching out,
your hand supporting us and your grace giving us strength.
Help us truly to believe that,
not just in our minds but also in our hearts;
to put our trust wholly in you,
confident that you will never fail us.
Help us to let go of the fears and anxieties that weigh us down,
that destroy our confidence and undermine our happiness,
that alienate us from others and prevent us living life to the full.
Help us to receive the freedom you offer,
which comes from knowing that you hold all things in your hands
and that nothing can finally separate us from your love.
In the name of Christ we ask it.
Amen.

475

Eternal God,
  we praise you for the faithfulness of your love
  and the constancy of your purpose.
We thank you that though all else may change,
  you stay the same;
  that though heaven and earth may pass away,
  your word endures for ever.
Teach us to live each moment in the light of that assurance,
  recognising that your promises in Christ will never fail
  and that the new life he has won for us will never fade.
Help us to enjoy all the many blessings of this life,
  celebrating everything you have so richly given,
  but help us finally to put our trust in your eternal kingdom,
  in the one hope that will never disappoint us,
  by the grace of Jesus Christ our Lord.
Amen.

476

Loving God,
  we thank you for your constant guidance throughout our lives,
  for the assurance that you are always there
  to encourage, strengthen and support us.
We praise you for the many ways we have found that to be true:
  the strength you have given in times of weakness,
  encouragement in times of fear,
  support in times of difficulty,
  faith in times of doubt.
Teach us through all we have experienced
  to trust you more completely in the future,
  confident that whatever may be asked of us,
  your hand will hold us firm and see us through.
Amen.

477

Lord Jesus Christ,
  forgive us for the way we have made our relationship with you one-sided,
  expecting you to be there for us
  but all too rarely being there for you.
Forgive us that we have let go of you so often,
  intent on going our own way,
  clinging to what ultimately can never satisfy.
Forgive us for doubting you when times are hard,
  questioning your ability to lead us safely through;
  for reaching out only when we have need of you,

asking you to lift us up from a mire of our own making
and to set us on our feet again.
Help us to hold on to you more firmly,
in simple trust,
quiet confidence
and eager expectation,
knowing that whatever we face
and wherever we may find ourselves,
you will never let go of us.
Amen.

478
Lord,
you call us to live by faith,
not by sight.
You tell us to trust in things unseen,
in realities we cannot grasp.
We do our best,
but it's not easy,
for we like to have everything cut and dried,
spelt out for us down to the finest detail.
We struggle to cope with uncertainties in relation to everyday matters,
the routine business of life,
let alone our eternal destiny.
Yet we know deep down that there is no other way,
for the joys you hold in store for us are beyond our imagining,
too awesome for the human mind to comprehend.
Teach us, then, to leave all things in your hands,
trusting for tomorrow through what we know of you today.
Teach us to work for your kingdom
until that day we enter into the wonder of your presence.
Amen.

479
Sovereign God,
we thank you that whatever we may face,
whatever dangers may threaten us,
you are able to deliver us from evil.
In life and in death you are by our side,
nothing able to separate us from the wonder of your love.
Help us, then, to trust you always,
to love you unswervingly
and to honour you each day with faithful and committed service,
to the glory of your name.
Amen.

480

Gracious God,
    we thank you for enabling us to know you,
    for calling us, by your grace, to share in your sovereign purpose.
We thank you that, though this call brings challenge as well as fulfilment,
    trials as well as blessing,
    you are always by our side,
    offering us the strength and encouragement we need
    to continue our journey.
For all the ways you have led us thus far,
    and for the guidance you shall yet give,
    receive our praise.
Help us to trust in your will,
    to respond to your summons,
    and to work always for your glory,
    this day and for evermore.
Amen.

481

Sovereign God,
    we thank you for all those over the centuries
    who have had the courage to take difficult decisions.
We think of the call of Abram to venture into the unknown,
    of Moses to confront the tyranny of Pharaoh,
    of David to take on the might of Goliath,
    of the prophets to declare your word despite hostility,
    of the disciples to leave all and follow Jesus,
    of Saul to turn from persecutor to ambassador of the Church.
We thank you for the determination and the courage these showed;
    their willingness to trust in you,
    coupled with their readiness to step out in faith,
    despite no guarantees as to what the future might hold.
Speak to us through their example
    and through your word,
    so that when decisions must be made
    we will be ready to make them,
    and equipped to choose the right path
    through Jesus Christ our Lord.
Amen.

482

Loving God,
    though we strive to keep faith
    there are times when we find that hard,
    testing and demanding circumstances causing us to doubt,
    throwing a shadow over everything we believe.

We question our ability to keep going in such moments,
    wondering what is happening to us,
    and though we look to you for assurance we do not find it.
Help us, when these times come,
    to remember that you have shared our humanity in Christ
    and that you therefore understand what we are facing.
Inspire us through the faith and courage he showed,
    and so help us to trust in your purpose
    even when we cannot see the way ahead.
In his name we pray.
Amen.

483
Loving God,
    it is hard sometimes to continue believing
    when so much denies our convictions.
It is harder still when those around us ridicule our faith
    and deride us for following you,
    and it is hardest of all when hopes are dashed
    and you seem far from us,
    our prayers for help seemingly unanswered.
Give us strength,
    despite adversity or disappointment,
    to stay true to you,
    trusting in your purpose,
    in the assurance that your way will finally prevail.
Amen.

_____ Truth, disturbing nature of _____

484
God of truth,
   you know us better than we know ourselves.
You search our hearts and minds,
   seeing us as we really are
   and confronting us with our true selves.
Forgive us that all too often we shy away from what is hard to accept,
   refusing to countenance anything that contradicts our self-image.
We find it so difficult to be honest,
   closing our ears to truths we would rather not hear.
We avoid those who challenge and disturb us,
   preferring instead those who soothe and flatter our ego.
Thank you for those with the rare gift of speaking the truth in love;
   those prepared to risk our resentment, retaliation or rejection
   not out of spite or vindictiveness
   but because they genuinely care
   and want to help us grow as individuals.
God of all,
   give us true humility and meekness of spirit,
   so that we may be ready to listen and examine ourselves;
   ready to ask searching questions about who we are,
   ready to face the truth and to change where necessary.
In Christ's name we ask it.
Amen.

485
Loving God,
   we claim to be seekers after truth,
   but the reality is that the truth sometimes scares us.
It probes too deeply into areas we prefer kept hidden;
   it challenges us in ways we find hard to deal with;
   it exposes issues we would rather not face.
Despite our fine-sounding words
   we are often less than honest with ourselves and with others.
Forgive us,
   and give us the courage and sensitivity we need
   both to face the truth and to speak it,
   in the name of Christ,
   the Way,
   the Truth,
   and the Life.
Amen.

486
Merciful God,
    it's not easy being honest with ourselves,
    for there are some things we prefer to keep hidden
    rather than face the disturbing truth.
Occasionally we may glimpse our darker side,
    but we push it away,
    attempting to deny its existence even to ourselves,
    but the knowledge of our weakness is always there,
    lurking in the shadows.
Help us, then, to open our hearts before you
    and to acknowledge our faults,
    in the knowledge that you gave your Son for us
    while we were yet sinners.
Cleanse,
    redeem,
    renew,
    restore,
    and, by your grace, help us to come to terms with the people we are,
    so that one day we might become the people you would have us be,
    through Jesus Christ our Lord.
Amen.

487
Gracious God,
    you speak to us in all kinds of ways,
    through all kinds of people;
    forgive us that we are sometimes closed to what you have to say.
We avoid that which challenges, disturbs or unsettles us,
    preferring to criticise and condemn rather than face the issues raised.
Forgive us that we shut our ears to what we don't agree with,
    rather than listen to another point of view;
    that we are reluctant to accept new and unfamiliar ideas,
    taking refuge instead in what is tried and trusted.
Forgive us that we can become so bogged down
    in what we think is right,
    so sure of our own convictions and set in our ways
    that we resent anything new.
Open our hearts to the living reality of Christ,
    our minds to the sweeping breath of your Holy Spirit,
    and our souls to all that you would do and say,
    in the name of Christ.
Amen.

488
Lord Jesus Christ,
   the Way, the Truth and the Life,
   forgive us the times we have kept you out of our lives,
   preferring to do our own thing in our own way
   and believing we have no need of your help.
Forgive the times we have kept you standing on the doorstep,
   not wanting to face your challenge
   or to have our comfortable lifestyle questioned by the truth.
Forgive the times we have welcomed you for a moment
   only to show you the door later,
   faith proving incompatible or hard to reconcile
   with certain aspects of our lives.
Help us to open the door of our hearts without reserve
   and to keep it open, come what may.
Come now and make your home in us
   so that we may dwell in you always,
   rejoicing in your love
   and celebrating your glorious gift of new life.
Amen.

489
Living God,
   it isn't easy to speak out against wrong.
We prefer to mind our own business rather than get involved;
   to keep our heads down
   for fear of the possible consequences should we intervene.
More than that, we hold back for fear of hypocrisy,
   being all too conscious of our own faults and failings,
   and so feeling that we have no right to judge others.
For good or bad reasons,
   from the best or worst of motives,
   we are sometimes silent,
   allowing evil to go unchallenged,
   rather than lifting up our voices against it.
Help us to know when it is not only right but necessary to speak,
   and when such moments come,
   give us wisdom, sensitivity and courage,
   so that we will know the words to say
   and be enabled to say them.
Give us that rare ability to speak the truth in love,
   through Jesus Christ our Lord.
Amen.

490
Lord Jesus Christ,
    we talk of following you
    but much of the time we expect you to follow us.
We want you to conform to our own wishes.
We ask you to meet our list of requirements.
We decide the way we want you to work,
    attempting to mould your purpose
    according to our own narrow horizons.
Lord Jesus Christ,
    break through the chains we put around you,
    and help us to face the searching nature of your truth
    and the challenge it daily brings.
Amen.

Wholeness and healing

491
Lord Jesus Christ,
   we remember today how, throughout your ministry,
   you looked to bring healing and wholeness.
We remember how you touched the lepers,
   restored sight to the blind,
   cured the sick,
   and helped the lame to walk;
   how you brought hope to the broken-hearted
   and those crushed in spirit,
   peace of mind to those who were troubled,
   and forgiveness to those burdened by guilt or failure.
Lord Jesus Christ,
   we bring before you all in any kind of need,
   praying again for your healing and renewing touch
   in body, mind and spirit,
   this and every day.
Restore us and make us whole,
   by your grace.
Amen.

492
Loving Lord,
   you are always looking to respond to our needs,
   constantly reaching out to touch our lives with your love,
   yet all too often we fail to seek the help you long to give us.
We trust in our own strength;
   we try this, that and everything else;
   and we only remember you when we reach the end of our tether
   and there is no one left to turn to.
Forgive us for relegating you to the periphery
   rather than putting you at the centre of our lives.
Forgive us for treating you as a last resort instead of a first recourse.
Teach us to bring our needs to you,
   knowing that, though you may not always respond as we want you to,
   you will always respond in love,
   providing for our needs,
   granting us peace
   and bringing us the wholeness that you alone can give.
In your name we ask it.
Amen.

_____ Will and purpose of God _____

see also Faithfulness of God; Guidance; Kingdom of God; Trust

493
Gracious God,
   help us always to remember that you are able to transform situations
   in a way beyond our expectations,
   overcoming obstacles,
   offering strength,
   equipping with gifts
   and shaping circumstances to make the impossible become possible.
Remind us of the innumerable ways you have acted across history,
   taking the most unlikely of people
   and using them in even unlikelier situations
   to make known your love and fulfil your purpose.
Save us, then, from closing our minds
   to the opportunities that you might present.
Teach us, in our turn, to be alert to your call
   and ready to respond wherever you might lead,
   to the glory of your name.
In Christ's name we ask it.
Amen.

494
Living God,
   we do not find it easy to live by faith.
We want some idea of what the future holds,
   some assurance that things will work out as we hope.
We like to feel in control of our lives,
   able to shape events and influence our circumstances.
Above all, we feel the need to plan,
   to make provisions for ourselves and our loved ones,
   to map out some kind of direction for our lives.
   so that we may make wise decisions for the future.
Yet our hold on life is so tenuous,
   what seems certain today under threat tomorrow,
   what seems ours one moment plucked from our grasp the next.
Help us, then, as we look ahead, to seek your guidance in all decisions,
   but teach us also to recognise that the future is ultimately in your hands,
   and so help us to seek your will before all else
   and to trust that, whatever life may bring,
   you will lead us safely through.
In Christ's name we ask it.
Amen.

495

Living God,
  we praise you for the assurance that your will shall be done
  and your purpose shall finally triumph.
We thank you that in all the changing circumstances of life
  you are constantly active,
  day by day working to fulfil your sovereign purpose.
Teach us, then, to live each moment with total confidence,
  knowing that, though all else may fail,
  you will not.
Teach us to leave all things in your hands,
  secure in your love,
  convinced of your faithfulness,
  and certain that what you have promised,
  you will deliver,
  through Jesus Christ our Lord.
Amen.

496

Living God,
  we thank you that you are always at work in our lives and in the world,
  constantly looking to fulfil your sovereign purpose.
Forgive us that all too often we leave it at that,
  expecting you to do everything
  and forgetting the part we have to play if your will is to be done.
Show us where you would have us serve,
  and help us to work with you for the growth of your kingdom
  and the sharing of your love,
  through Jesus Christ our Lord.
Amen.

497

Living God,
  we thank you that you are always at work,
  striving to establish your kingdom and to enfold all things in your love.
We praise you for the way you work in our lives –
  guiding,
  teaching,
  enabling,
  equipping –
  constantly looking to draw us closer to yourself.
But we thank you also that you have given us free will:
  the ability to make our own decisions
  and to respond knowingly to your love.

Forgive us when we abuse that freedom,
   flouting your commandments
   and deliberately going against the purpose
   that you have revealed in Christ.
Forgive us when the decisions we take
   contradict our faith and deny the gospel.
Take our lives,
   with all the mistakes we have made and continue to make,
   and work within and through us towards the fulfilment of your will,
   to the glory of your name.
Amen.

498

Lord Jesus Christ,
   it is hard sometimes not to feel overwhelmed
   by the scale of the challenges we face
   and the obstacles that block our path.
We are part of a world where faith is ridiculed
   and where your name is casually dismissed;
   a world in which people live for today with no thought of tomorrow
   and in which good seems overpowered by evil.
Instead of truth, there is falsehood;
   instead of love, hatred;
   instead of peace, division;
   instead of joy, sorrow;
   the dawn of your kingdom apparently further away than ever
   rather than drawing near.
Teach us, despite everything, not to lose heart.
Help us to understand that we have a part to play
   in fulfilling your purpose
   but that the final victory is down to you.
Give us strength to do what you ask of us as best we can
   and then to leave the rest in your hands,
   confident that, though we may not see it,
   the seed you have sown is growing,
   and that the day will come when you will rule with the Father
   in your eternal kingdom –
   one God,
   world without end.
Amen.

499

Lord Jesus Christ,
   we claim to serve you
   but all too easily we slip into serving ourselves.

Instead of listening to *your* voice
   we tell ourselves what *we* want to hear.
Instead of seeking *your* will
   we prefer our *own*,
   expecting you to conform to *our* expectations.
Forgive us all the ways,
   consciously and unconsciously,
   that we shut our minds to your living presence,
   to anything we would rather not see or hear.
Break through our narrow vision
   and help us to encounter you as you really are.
So may we truly know you,
   genuinely love you
   and faithfully serve you,
   today and every day,
   to the glory of your name.
Amen.

500

Sovereign God,
   Lord of past, present and future,
   we thank you that in all the uncertainties of life
   we find in you one who is unchanging:
   a rock on which we can base our lives,
   a fortress to protect us in times of danger
   and a shield to defend us in the journey of life.
We praise you that nothing can ever overcome your purpose;
   that whatever may fight against you,
   your will shall finally triumph.
In that assurance may we face each day,
   confident that you will deliver us from evil
   and lead us safely through into your eternal kingdom,
   through Jesus Christ our Lord.
Amen.

501

Sovereign God,
   we can't help wondering sometimes about the fairness of life.
When we see the good suffer and the wicked prosper,
   our faith is shaken and we inevitably start to question.
There is so much that doesn't seem to make sense;
   so much that appears to deny everything we believe about you.
Teach us, despite the apparent contradictions of life,
   to keep faith that you are there,
   striving against everything that frustrates your will
   and denies your love.

Teach us to hold on to those moments when we see wrongs righted
and justice done.
Above all, teach us to look at the cross of Christ
and to draw strength from the victory you won there
over what had seemed to be the triumph of evil.
Amen.

___ Wisdom and foolishness of God ___

502
Living God,
    we do not risk much today in committing ourselves to you,
    yet we still do not find it easy,
    for there are many who pour scorn on the gospel,
    who ridicule Christianity,
    and who mock those who profess faith in you.
Still more are dismissive of you;
    not hostile
    but simply regarding Christian teaching
    and everything to do with the Church
    as an outdated irrelevance.
In some ways we find such apathy and indifference harder to cope with
    than outright rejection,
    for none of us likes being thought foolish,
    and as a result we are tempted to compromise our convictions,
    to tone down our message or even to conceal our commitment.
Help us to remember that your wisdom
    is often counted by the world as foolishness,
    and to remember in turn that the wisdom of this world
    is all too often folly.
Give us the courage and dedication we need to stay true to you
    no matter what people may say or think –
    the faith, if necessary, to be fools for Christ.
Amen.

503
Gracious God,
    your way can sometimes seem like foolishness –
    the way of sacrifice and self-denial,
    of love in the face of hatred,
    faithfulness in the face of rejection.
In the eyes of the world
    the message of Christ crucified continues to look like folly,
    but to us it is a revelation of your power and wisdom,
    a demonstration of your mercy,
    and the most marvellous expression of your saving grace.
Teach us to show our gratitude not just through words
    but through following his way,
    ready in turn to be fools for Christ.
Amen.

504

Loving God,
  we thank you for all there is to explore
  in this wonderful world and fascinating universe you have given us.
We thank you for all those whose study and research
  have unlocked so many of the secrets
  concerning the origins and development of life,
  and we thank you that you have given us minds
  with which to think, enquire and learn.
Teach us to apply ourselves to gaining understanding,
  but teach us also that, however much we may learn,
  true wisdom concerning ultimate realities lies not in human ingenuity,
  but in you,
  the beginning and end of all.
Amen.

505

Loving God,
  you call us to distinctive discipleship,
  a way of life that sets us apart from others:
  not a self-righteous superiority based on judgemental intolerance,
  but a quality of love and a willingness to serve
  that shows itself in everything we say and do.
Forgive us that we fall so far short of that calling,
  compromising what we believe for fear of mockery.
Forgive us that we go along with the way of the crowd
  rather than follow the demanding way of Christ.
Speak to us now,
  challenge our complacency,
  and give us courage to be different.
Amen.

Witnessing to Christ

see also Faith: Faith in action

506

Lord Jesus Christ,
   just as others have introduced you to us,
   so help us in turn to introduce you to others:
   not preaching at them,
   nor seeking to ram our beliefs down their throats,
   nor trying to argue with them
   or to convince them of the claims of the gospel,
   but simply pointing at who and what you are.
Help us to speak of all that you mean to us
   and of everything we have found you to be,
   and so may others come to meet you
   and know you for themselves,
   through your grace.
Amen.

507

Lord Jesus Christ,
   you call us,
   as you call all your people,
   to go out and proclaim the gospel.
You expect us not simply to believe the good news,
   but also to share it.
Forgive us for failing to honour that calling;
   for being only too ready to come to you
   but less willing to go out in your name;
   eager to receive
   but reluctant to give.
Help us to recognise our responsibility towards others –
   to understand that if we leave it to someone else
   to tell them about Jesus,
   they may never hear the good news.
Help us to understand that discipleship without service
   is no discipleship at all,
   and that faith without witness
   is a denial of everything we claim to believe.
Fill us, then, with new vision and resolve,
   so that when the opportunity comes to speak for you,
   we may do so –
   faithfully,

honestly,
sensitively
and joyfully –
to the glory of your name.
Amen.

508

Lord Jesus Christ,
    you have called us to be your witnesses,
    to proclaim your name and make known your love,
    but, though we try to respond to that challenge,
    we find it so hard.
When we speak of you we are met with indifference,
    even hostility.
Though we keep on trying,
    in our hearts we give up,
    no longer expecting lives to be changed by your word.
Teach us to look beyond appearances
    and to recognise that, though we may not always see it,
    the seed we may sow bears fruit in unexpected ways and places;
    that though much will fall on barren soil,
    some will find fertile ground
    and in the fullness of time bear a rich harvest.
Help us to trust not in our ability
    but in your life-giving power,
    confident that, if *we* play our part,
    you will play yours.
In your name we ask it.
Amen.

509

Lord Jesus Christ,
    you have called us to bear witness to what you have done
    and on occasions there come opportunities to do just that.
You don't expect us to be gifted evangelists,
    but you do ask us to speak naturally of you
    when the chance presents itself.
Yet, more often than we care to remember,
    when that time has come we have wasted it,
    uncertain what to say,
    worried about making fools of ourselves,
    afraid of being misunderstood.
Forgive us all the occasions we have let you down,
    failing to share the joy we have found in you.
Teach us to reflect on your goodness,

to recognise all you have done for us,
and so to make the most of every opportunity you give us
to proclaim your love and make known the good news.
In your name we ask it.
Amen.

510
Lord of all,
    you call us to witness to Christ;
    to share with others what he has done for us.
Help us to do that wisely,
    sensitively,
    honestly
    and faithfully.
Teach us to speak from personal experience
    rather than by empty rote,
    to present the simple message of the gospel
    rather than the intricacies of doctrine or dogma,
    and to be conscious of those we are talking to,
    instead of conscious of ourselves.
Whenever and wherever the opportunity presents itself,
    teach us to witness in a way that is relevant and alive,
    and so may your love be made known to all,
    in the name of Christ.
Amen.

511
God of all,
    we talk much about witness, evangelism and mission,
    about sharing the good news
    and being a light to the nations,
    but, when it comes to it,
    our words are rarely backed up by actions.
We focus instead on worship,
    prayer,
    private devotion,
    on personal growth and times of fellowship,
    our minds turned in on the Church rather than out to the world.
Forgive us our lack of faith,
    our lack of courage and our lack of vision.
Give us the words to say and the will to speak them,
    and, above all,
    grant us a life that in every part proclaims your glory
    and tells of your love,
    through Jesus Christ our Lord.
Amen.

512
Lord,
   it is hard to share our faith with a *few*,
   let alone *many*.
When we listen to your call to be witnesses to the ends of the earth
   we feel that the task is hopelessly beyond us,
   our resources feebly inadequate to meet the challenge.
Yet that is to view things from our perspective rather than yours,
   for you do not leave us dependent on our strength
   but rather equip us with the power of the Holy Spirit
   who is able to work in ways far exceeding our expectations.
Move within us,
   as you have moved in your people across the centuries,
   and teach us to trust you for the help we need,
   when we need it.
In the name of Christ we pray.
Amen.

513
Sovereign God,
   you have given us so much to share,
   more than we can ever begin to express.
You have showered us with your blessings,
   touching our lives in innumerable ways.
You have given us joy that knows no bounds,
   mercy beyond all our deserving,
   hope that can never be exhausted,
   peace that passes understanding
   and love that exceeds anything we can ever ask or think of.
Teach us to share that with others,
   to tell joyfully and spontaneously of everything you have done
   and of all you mean to us,
   to the glory of your name.
Amen.

Word of God

see also Call of God

514

Gracious God,
    we praise you for the way your word has spoken
    to so many across the years,
    offering a lamp for their path and a faith to live by.
We thank you for the way it has spoken to us,
    stirring our imagination,
    kindling and nurturing faith,
    confronting and questioning,
    yet also renewing and uplifting,
    each day assuring us of your constant love and gracious purpose.
Teach us to study your word,
    to reflect on its meaning,
    and to seek enlightenment,
    so that we may hear your voice and respond.
Open our hearts and minds to what you would say to us,
    and help us to listen.
In Jesus' name we pray.
Amen.

515

Gracious God,
    you have spoken through the Law and Prophets,
    through words of wisdom, history and the psalms,
    through the testimony of Evangelists and Apostles to Jesus Christ,
    and above all through the Word made flesh.
We praise you that we can turn to the Bible whenever we wish to
    and read it freely in our own tongue.
We can read new translations that help bring the age-old message to life,
    and we have access to all kinds of resources
    designed to deepen our understanding of what we read.
Forgive us that all too often we leave your word sitting on a shelf,
    unopened,
    unexplored.
Help us to recognise the priceless treasure you have given us
    in the Scriptures,
    and teach us, in the clamour of each day,
    to make time to read them, reverently and thoughtfully,
    so that your voice may speak again,
    offering light to our path and the way to life in all its fullness.
Amen.

516
Living God,
  you have given your word in the Scriptures
  but, all too often, we fail to read them.
We dip in casually as the mood takes us,
  selecting those passages that suit us best
  and ignoring any that might prove difficult or demanding.
Even the little we read is rarely applied to our lives
  in a way that really touches us.
Despite the claims we make for it,
  much of the Bible is a closed book to us.
Forgive us,
  and help us to make time and space to study your word,
  to hear you speaking,
  and to respond in faith.
Amen.

517
Loving God,
  we thank you for the way your word has spoken
  across the centuries
  and the way it continues to speak today.
We praise you that the gospel has changed the lives
  of innumerable individuals,
  and that it has changed our lives in turn.
Teach us never to lose sight of that message
  or its transforming power;
  never to forget that, however familiar it may be,
  it can still speak in new and exciting ways
  to our hearts and our daily experience.
Remind us of that truth, day by day,
  so that we may read it with hope, faith and expectation,
  hearing your voice,
  discerning your will,
  receiving your strength
  and responding to your call.
Amen.